ON
CRITICAL
RACE
THEORY

ON
CRITICAL
RACE
THEORY

WHY IT MATTERS &
WHY YOU SHOULD CARE

VICTOR RAY

RANDOM HOUSE
New York

Published in the United States by Random House, an imprint and
division of Penguin Random House LLC, New York.

RANDOM HOUSE and the HOUSE colophon are registered
trademarks of Penguin Random House LLC.

Hardcover ISBN: 9780593446447
Ebook ISBN: 9780593446454

Printed in the United States of America on acid-free paper

randomhousebooks.com

9 8 7 6 5 4 3 2 1

First Edition

Book design by Debbie Glasserman

For Louise, Malcolm,
Pam, and Raymond

CONTENTS

PREFACE

It has been reported that Malcolm X once said that if you have no critics, you'll likely have no success. If indeed having critics is the key to success, then critical race theorists have every reason to be wildly optimistic.

KIMBERLÉ CRENSHAW[1]

I was two years old the first time the cops were called on my family. At a parade in downtown Pittsburgh, my uncle Harold lifted me to his shoulders so I could see over the crowd. His behaving as loving uncles do led someone to jump to the conclusion that my dark-skinned uncle had abducted a light-skinned toddler. They told the police. Kidnappers aren't known for taking stolen children to parades, or anywhere with large crowds. Nonetheless, the police questioned my uncle, letting us go when they were satisfied that we were family. Variations of this scene repeated throughout my life, from infancy to the present. When I was about ten, a white woman driving past our trailer called the police on my dad for playing with me in the yard, again criminalizing family joy. When we were teenagers, white clerks followed my brother around stores where I walked unbothered. Questioning (and threatening) stares still occasionally greet my mixed-race family as we go about normal tasks. Even now, when my family gets together, we are sometimes asked if, and how, we know each other.

My experiences with racism reflect aspects of America's broader racial system. The assumption that my uncle and I weren't family is tied to our nation's peculiar racial categorization system, with its singular "one-drop" rule and its long history of bans on interracial marriage. Such bans would have outlawed my parents' union and were intended to prevent my birth.[2] Assuming my Black male caretakers were dangerous and deviant, rather than loving and conscientious, reflects the routine criminalization of Black people's family lives and gendered stereotypes about Black masculinity. And as a seemingly endless series of videos of police violence against unarmed Black men has shown, calling the police and falsely accusing a Black man of stealing a child put lives at risk, regardless of the fact of innocence.

By connecting individual experiences to broader patterns of racial inequality, stories like mine have shaped critical race theory. Critical race theory recognizes that narratives influence our understanding of the world and uses stories as an empathetic bridge across racial divides. Stories can help outsiders understand and connect with the unfairness, capriciousness, and cruelty of racism. Critical race theorists recognize that narratives may not, in and of themselves, be compelling evidence. So they couple stories with meticulous research highlighting America's profound racial inequality, showing how race and racism shape people's lives. By highlighting the stories of how people of color navigate and survive American racism, critical race theory provides perspectives often conspicuously absent from mainstream books, movies, and media. One reason I'm writing this book is that people are trying to erase and turn back the relatively minor inroads critical race theorists have made in getting these stories told.

I was introduced to critical race theory as an undergrad at Vassar College when I transferred there from the Borough of Manhattan Community College (BMCC). Contrary to the idea of colleges as radicalizing institutions, my introduction to critical race theory was more confirmation than revelation. I enrolled at BMCC right after 9/11, when, like many New Yorkers, I reevaluated my life. BMCC was just blocks away from the World Trade Center and the college had lost students during the attack. When I started taking classes there in February 2002, the college served a broad swath of New Yorkers and students from all over the world. I quickly became involved in student government and anti-racist organizing, doing things like testifying at City Hall against tuition increases for some of New York's poorest students. After two years I moved to Vassar, a small liberal arts college in upstate New York. The contrast between these two schools was intense, and it was clear to me that they were preparing people for different places in the social hierarchy. Despite the glaring resource differences between these schools, I watched administrators at both use similar tactics to avoid meeting antiracist student demands for things that racial justice activists have been fighting for since the 1960s.[3]

My personal history primed me to understand critical race theory because I had witnessed the highly variable treatment received by my family members of different hues. Because I am often read as white, I heard the ways white people, thinking they were alone, sometimes spoke about people of color. These interactions included the relatively subdued (but nonetheless harmful) racism that's common in American culture, like asking if I felt safe living near Black people, or "jokes" about the supposed inferiority of Black culture or language.[4] Sometimes these comments included more blatant racism, like being told Black folks in a fancy car must be drug dealers, or when a white Vassar student suggested that the cultural center for students of color should be torn down and replaced with "whites only" parking. Scholars have documented differences in whites' talk about race in public and private, with considerably more animus and casual racism employed in what they call the "white backstage."[5] When I read the foundational critical race theory article "Whiteness as Property" (see chapter 6), which used passing as a launchpad to explore America's history of racial plunder, I knew I had found an intellectual home.

The vast resource gap between BMCC and Vassar also left me with the sense that the superficial explanations for racial inequality I had previously been taught were at best wrong, and at worst intentionally misleading. Personal ill feelings, or the caricatured backward racist, couldn't explain the callousness of social policies designed to target and shorten Black life. I was also bothered by the racial liberalism I encountered among some Vassar students—a kind of smug paternalism that assumed white folks knew what was best for people of color. I knew that after graduation these students and their paternalism were going to run things in business, the media, and politics. I sometimes felt that although I could (but didn't) pass for white, I was still the blackest person some of these students had sustained interactions with.

Critical race theory also appealed to me because it critiqued inadequate explanations of racial inequality across the political spectrum. Critical race theorists skewered the Right's overt hostility to people of color, evident in explicitly anti-immigrant and anti-Black policy prescriptions. Critical race theorists also criticized liberals' tepid acceptance of diversity on unequal terms, such as organizational policies that avoid confronting racialized power and resource differences in the workplace.[6] Analytic tools developed by critical race theorists showed how colorblind racism—where warring political camps met and compromised—facilitated laws like the 1994 Violent Crime Control and Law Enforcement Act that were discriminatory in outcome, if race neutral in form.[7] Once I learned the core concepts developed by these critiques, I had a language to describe and understand the sometimes-hidden processes of discrimination, exclusion, and structural racism that shape the social world. I learned that race was a social construction that helped to explain the peculiar history shaping my racial identity. (Spoiler: that history shaped your racial identity, too.) The concept of structural racism allowed me to see how race is used to divvy up resources from classrooms to boardrooms, sometimes intentionally but sometimes as a by-product of "nonracial" actions. In other words, ideas from critical race theory did exactly what good ideas are supposed to do, allowing me to better see, understand, and navigate the world.

This book spreads these good ideas, making key concepts from critical race theory accessible to a broad audience. Social theorists often convey ideas in complex technical language. For those new to the conversation, such language can obscure as much as it illuminates. In 2020, political opponents of critical race theory used its relative obscurity and specialized language to misrepresent the goals of the idea. Somewhat improbably, these opponents have made the niche intellectual tradition I work in—work that is usually confined to academic journals and lecture halls—part of a moral panic over antiracism in the United States. Rather than a body of serious scholarship about the causes and consequences of racial inequality, critical race theory has been caricatured by these opponents as a dangerous and scary straw man. This caricature is unintelligible to those familiar with the enormous body of research on the history and current reality of structural racism in the United States.

As a person committed to antiracism, I would prefer it if opponents of racial equality hadn't chosen to attack research aimed at diagnosing and healing racial inequality. It's not coincidental that the conservative think tanks promoting the anti–critical race theory hysteria tend to support policies that strike at the heart of civil rights victories—making it harder for people of color to vote,[8] undermining public education,[9] and promoting nativist and anti-immigrant policies such as militarizing the border. These conservative think tanks, by and large, also supported a would-be authoritarian president whose political rise was facilitated by the slander of birtherism, an unhinged conspiracy theory questioning President Barack Obama's citizenship.[10] Like former president Donald Trump, the groups promoting the anti–critical race theory moral panic aren't interested in solving racial inequality; they are manipulating racism for political advantage.

Authoritarian movements always target ideas and intellectuals that question the legitimacy of the social hierarchy upon which their worldview is built. For long swaths of U.S. history, both mainstream political parties tacitly (or openly) supported racial authoritarianism. Recent history has shown that many white Americans are willing to rally around a political candidate who promoted nostalgia for the era of open white supremacy in America. This book joins several recent volumes outlining the growing threat the authoritarian Right poses for democracy. First, Timothy Snyder's *On Tyranny: Twenty Lessons from the Twentieth Century* provides a field guide through the Trump era by way of an intellectual time machine, showing how the history of twentieth-century authoritarianism resonates with contemporary American politics.[11] Similarly, Jason Stanley's *How Fascism Works: The Politics of Us and Them* shows how fascist tropes—such as an unthinking commitment to social hierarchy and racialized conceptions of law and order—have animated the American center and Far Right.[12] Critical race theory has long recognized that authoritarianism, racial fascism, and antidemocratic politics are not abstractions for people of color in America.

While I wish the attacks on critical race theory were intellectually honest, they have nonetheless provided an opportunity to present the ideas on their own terms. Those terms include accurately describing the roots of America's racial problems to find a collective fix. Research on political identity and polarization shows that in some cases, providing evidence of racial inequality in the criminal justice system can *increase* support for racially unequal laws.[13] This research helps me recognize that a book like this, which synthesizes a fraction of the clear empirical evidence of structural racism in American life, is not for everyone. Some people will never be convinced by a multiracial professor's book about scholarship that has been widely demonized and mischaracterized. So I'm not writing to those folks.

I'm writing to people acting in good faith, looking for an accessible primer on some of the most influential and essential concepts developed by critical race theorists. Critical race theory is being targeted because it is an effective, useful, and potentially accessible body of scholarship that everyone interested in creating an antiracist, just future should access. I present the concepts and supporting evidence with fidelity to their academic roots. I hope this book reaches people genuinely committed to racial equality.

WHY CRITICAL RACE THEORY MATTERS

The law, in its majestic equality, forbids rich and poor alike to
sleep under bridges, to beg in the streets, and to steal their bread.

ANATOLE FRANCE[1]

WHAT IS CRITICAL RACE THEORY?

"Not everything that is faced can be changed; but nothing
can be changed until it is faced."[2] James Baldwin wrote
those words to convey the intellectual's role in laying bare
a nation's faults. Critical race theory is a body of scholarship
that faces America's brutal racial history, recognizes the
parts of that history that remain unchanged, and works
toward changing the rest.

Racism is America's central political fault line. Critical
race theory shows how this fault line runs through the
American legal system. Critical race theory developed, in
part, to explain why the monumental legal victories of

the civil rights movement—for instance, the *Brown v. Board of Education* decision outlawing state-sponsored school segregation—didn't always lead to lasting improvements in the lives of people of color in the United States.[3] By the late seventies and early eighties it was clear that a backlash to the civil rights movement was gaining traction. Several trends supported this conclusion. Schools that had been forced to open their doors to Black students in the wake of the *Brown* ruling were resegregating. This resegregation continues, with some public schools now equally or more segregated than before *Brown*.[4] The best evidence shows that discrimination against Black men in entry-level jobs hasn't decreased since the late 1980s, and emerging businesses are increasingly segregated.[5] The impact of antidiscrimination law in the workplace is also waning (or reversing) as occupational desegregation stalled in the 1980s.[6] Conservative think tanks waged an all-out war on affirmative action in higher education, characterizing policies designed to (slightly) intervene in decades of explicit exclusion from white colleges as reverse racism.[7] It might be tempting to diagnose policies like affirmative action and school desegregation as failures because racial equality is still elusive in schools and workplaces. But these policies successfully opened educational opportunities and jobs that were formerly closed to most Black Americans. Policies designed to create racial equality weren't targeted by white hostility because they didn't work. They were targeted because they *did*.

Hoping to explain the backlash to the civil rights victories, a group of law students and legal scholars—including Kimberlé Crenshaw, Richard Delgado, Mari Matsuda, Patricia Williams, Kendall Thomas, Phillip T. Nash, and Neil Gotanda, among others—turned to the writings of Derrick Bell, a gifted lawyer who worked on landmark civil rights cases and wrote a pathbreaking casebook on race and the law.[8] Bell was the first tenured Black professor at Harvard Law School, but his considerable personal achievements never clouded his vision of collective struggle as the terrain on which individual plaudits are built. After years of protesting over Harvard Law's refusal to hire more faculty of color, Bell left, and "the School suffered a 100% reduction in its tenured minority faculty."[9]

Despite Bell's monumental contributions to the larger civil rights struggle, stagnating and reversing racial progress led him to question the ultimate efficacy of the movement's legal strategy. Bell worried that his work was contributing to what the historian Jelani Cobb called "a more durable system of segregation," as new forms of seemingly race-neutral exclusion emerged to undermine civil rights gains.[10]

Bell began to critique the intellectual underpinnings of the civil rights movement he contributed to, arguing that

structural racism was malleable, intractable, and a consti-
tutive feature of American law. Drawing on Bell's work,
and in reaction to the critical legal studies movement, these
burgeoning critical race theorists critiqued existing explanations of the relationship between race and the law as inadequate to understand racial backlash and enduring racial
inequality. Critical legal scholars argued that, despite its
neutral pretensions, the law was a tool of the economically
powerful. But critical legal scholars largely ignored how
race shaped legal precedent. Critical race theorists extended
this critique, showing how the law often forwarded white
prerogatives. After all, members of the judiciary claimed
that the law remained racially neutral while deciding what
fraction of blood made one white or Black or Indian.[11] The
judiciary claimed no bias while divvying up ballot access,
the rights protected by suffrage, or access to citizenship.
The judiciary claimed impartiality while allowing neighborhoods and cities to segregate schools and hoard resources. And courts claimed to fairly decide what evidence
juries could see in discrimination cases where employees
were called by racial slurs, or co-workers hung nooses on
colleagues' desks. Rather than seeing the law as separate
from racial power—a neutral arbiter or umpire just calling
balls and strikes—these critical race theorists understood
the law as a tool that *occasionally* empowered people of
color but usually advanced whites' racial interests.

Since critical race theory's genesis as an insurgent intellectual movement in the late 1970s, the framework has spread beyond legal scholarship to parts of the social sciences and humanities. Although the theory developed as a critique of the veneer of race neutrality in the law, critical race legal theorists developed a broad framework for thinking about race. This framework includes foundational social science concepts—that race is a social construction, racism is primarily structural, social life is made up of intersecting identities. They also developed techniques that remain more contested, such as critical race theorists' use of narratives and parables to explain the impact of racial inequality. Critical race theory builds upon ideas that were central to and often developed by Black activist scholars— borrowing and formalizing these concepts into general descriptions that were easy to apply to related fields. Many of the intellectual precursors of critical race theory also shaped related intellectual traditions. For instance, W.E.B. Du Bois, the towering intellectual and first Black Harvard PhD, is a foundational figure in the disciplines of African American studies, sociology, and history. Race shapes social life, so it makes sense that social science and humanities disciplines share basic assumptions about the impact of race and racism. Kimberlé Crenshaw, who has been credited with coining the term "critical race theory," claims the framework is a "verb" because it is a broadly adaptable attempt to explain how racism is produced and maintained.[12]

Critics have treated this intellectual cross-fertilization

as evidence of a nefarious attempt to take over classrooms. These critics misunderstand how academic exchange works, with ideas regularly crossing porous disciplinary boundaries. Many of the ideas attributed to critical race theory are in fact just plain honesty about America's long-standing structural racism. Historians who study urban development and sociologists who study contemporary patterns of segregation may both conclude that racism is a structural feature of cities manifested in unequal work locations, access to housing, or commute times, and even in where environmental toxins are most likely to show up.[13] These scholars reach these conclusions not because they are critical race theorists but because a dispassionate examination of the evidence makes such conclusions hard to ignore.

WHITE BACKLASH IS ALSO A RACIAL RECKONING[14]

Given its roots as an insurgent intellectual framework explaining racial retrenchment, critical race theory became a perfect target for contemporary racist backlash. The Black Lives Matter protests following George Floyd's murder in 2020 were the largest civil rights protests in American history, with record numbers of white Americans expressing support for Black Lives Matter.[15] The scale, demands, and impact of these protests rattled contemporary guardians of the racial status quo. Following the protests, antiracist books topped bestseller lists, sports teams dropped racist names and mascots, and colleges and universities (once again) stated their commitments to diversity. Corporate public relations departments were not immune to these political pressures, with companies like Quaker Oats dropping the stereotypical images such as Aunt Jemima (which they had used for over a century). In the years since George Floyd was murdered, the idea that the country experienced a reckoning became almost cliché.

White backlash is also a reckoning. Historically, backlashes have attempted to roll back progress created by progressive social movements. The anti–critical race theory moral panic is part of a contemporary backlash. White parents protested physical desegregation following the civil rights movement and now some white parents are protesting a perceived slight desegregation of the curriculum in response to Black Lives Matter.

Racial ignorance is central to the current moral panic, but as a number of scholars have shown, some white Americans work hard to maintain their ignorance of racial reality.[16] In one of his many classic articles, the critical race philosopher Dr. Charles Mills asks us to "imagine an ignorance that resists. Imagine an ignorance that fights back."[17] Ignorance of America's racial history and of the causes of present-day racial inequality is a primary weapon in the current attacks on critical race theory. Former president Trump's claim that critical race theory was destroying the fabric of America, and white parents tearfully protesting a body of scholarship that is by and large not taught in elementary schools, are ignorance fighting back.

The state legislatures outlawing the teaching of critical race theory are trying to legally mandate racial ignorance by banning discussions of structural racism. According to *Education Week,* at the time of this writing "41 states have introduced bills or taken other steps" that target the teaching of critical race theory or curtail discussions of racism and sexism in the classroom.[18] Some of the laws don't explicitly mention critical race theory, but public statements from state legislators and governors often indicate that critical race theory—and ideas that opponents conflate with critical race theory, like diversity programs and white privilege—are the target. The goal of these laws is to make talking about the structural causes of racial inequality more difficult. The impact of these laws is already being felt, as there are reports of classes being canceled, conservative groups filing freedom of information requests for syllabi, increased targeted harassment of professors, and a general chilling effect among scholars who teach about race and ethnicity.

A number of bitter ironies are lost on those attacking critical race theory. First, the legislation spawned by this moral panic attempts to outlaw discussions of racism that make some white Americans uncomfortable. Outlawing teaching about racial inequality ironically confirms critical race theory's central claim that aspects of American law are

entwined with racism. Second, critical race theorists ana-
lyze dog whistles—racially coded language like Ronald Reagan's infamous "welfare queen"—that emerged to signal
racial animus once explicit slurs became taboo. The moral
panic has, in some quarters, turned "critical race theory"
itself into a dog whistle that stands in for a host of alleged
pathologies associated with people of color. Third, many
critics who claim that critical race theory is "tear[ing] apart
a national fabric" are conceding the point that racism is
central to American history.[19] To the extent that racism is
woven into the American fabric, this is true, as critical race
theory aims to get it out. Critical race theory doesn't want
to destroy America, but it does want to squarely reckon
with the way American racism has destroyed lives.

Leading critics of critical race theory are operating in
bad faith. Bad faith is hard to intuit, because sincerely held
political differences can invoke strong emotions and re-
solving conflict often requires trust in an opponent's honesty. But the leading promoter of the anti–critical race
theory moral panic, Christopher Rufo, explained the bad
faith of the strategy himself. Rufo is a failed candidate for
Seattle City Council and a former employee of the Discov-
ery Institute (a group that promotes intelligent design in
schools as an alternative to evolutionary theory) who has
been credited with taking the moral panic mainstream.[20]
According to The Washington Post, Rufo took to Twitter and
announced the plan:

We have successfully frozen their brand—"critical race theory"—into the public conversation and are steadily driving up negative perceptions. We will eventually turn it toxic, as we put all of the various cultural insanities under that brand category. . . . The goal is to have the public read something crazy in the newspaper and immediately think "critical race theory." We have decodified the term and will recodify it to annex the entire range of cultural constructions that are unpopular with Americans.[21]

The goal here isn't to inspire reflection or clarify the causes of racial inequality. Rather, by conflating a host of ideas conservative activists don't like—diversity, white privilege, antiracism—with critical race theory, they hope to induce an almost Pavlovian rejection of thought and replace it with anger to inspire the conservative base.

Somewhat paradoxically, part of taking these attacks seriously means not attempting to directly refute or debunk many of the lies about critical race theory spread by bad-faith actors. The history of prior racist movements is instructive here. According to Linda Gordon, during the second rise of the Ku Klux Klan in the 1920s, some in the media thought that exposing the Klan would help hobble the movement. Accordingly, the New York *World* published a national exposé of the Klan. Of course, many found the Klan repulsive. Nonetheless, engagement from the mainstream press *increased* Klan membership as their ideas were spread and seemingly legitimated.[22] More recently, mainstream publications like *The New York Times* and left-of-center magazines like *Mother Jones* refused to learn from this history, interviewing and profiling media-savvy members of the so-called "alt-right," and in the process helping to mainstream their ideology.[23] Movements opposed to racial equality recognize that publicity—regardless of the truth of the claims—can potentially bring them converts. Purveyors of the current moral panic around critical race theory aren't concerned with accurately representing scholarly claims—they want engagement that confers public legitimacy and allows them to further muddy the waters about the causes of racial inequality. This book is not an act of debunking, and it doesn't give bad-faith critics the attention and legitimacy they desperately crave but don't deserve.

CRITICAL RACE THEORY SHOWS HOW RACE HAS BEEN FOUNDATIONAL TO THE LAW

Racial slavery shaped America's Constitution, and the nation's early democratic pretensions belie the reality that the republic was a slaveocracy.[24] Democracy for white men was premised, in part, on Black enslavement. The Constitution's infamous three-fifths compromise added a proportion of Southern states' enslaved populations (who were not considered citizens and could not vote) to the enslavers' national political power. This compromise over Black lives paid immediate political dividends, with twelve of the nation's first eighteen presidents holding fellow humans as their property.[25] Early presidents recognized and worried about the destabilizing role of racial conflict. In his *Notes on the State of Virginia,* which was widely read in early U.S. history, Thomas Jefferson claimed Black people were unassimilable. He thought that the fledgling nation would likely be riven by a race war if Black people weren't deported "beyond the reach of mixture." Before becoming the Great Emancipator, Abraham Lincoln echoed Jefferson, and fantasized that sending Black Americans to Africa would help solve at least one of the country's race problems.[26]

Racism also shapes America's immigration laws. America's first immigration law, the 1790 Naturalization Act, limited citizenship to "free white persons." Just perusing the names of subsequent immigration laws, such as the Chinese Exclusion Act or the Asiatic Barred Zone Act, one is struck by the brazenly racial terminology, relics from a time before lawmakers were compelled to cloak their exclusionary goals. Instead, modern anti-immigration policy uses plausibly deniable language about cultural or linguistic differences.

Eugenicist thought heavily influenced immigration policy, most notably in the Immigration Act of 1924, which created "a hierarchy of desirability" for Europeans hoping to move to the United States.[27] The eugenics movement, which feared "racial degeneracy" and "mongrelization" if the national stock was diluted by "undesirable" immigrants, suborned science and policy to their goals of racial purity. Although eugenics is now considered a pseudoscience, the movement was helmed by esteemed scientists of the time. These researchers claimed the mantle of objectivity while using their credentials and the imprimatur of the world's top universities to launder scientific racism.[28] The 1924 law drew on eugenics, making Asians ineligible for citizenship. The law also created strict national-origin quotas, setting a specific cap on immigrants from each country. Lawmakers based these quotas upon the percentage of foreign-born residents in the United States in the 1890 census, not the 1910 census. Because it used the 1890 census data, the law excluded more people whom legislators considered undesirable.[29]

Although the 1924 Immigration Act studiously avoided using the word "race," the law's intent was clear to observers and imitators. In *Mein Kampf,* Hitler claimed that the United States' race-based immigration policy was superior to Germany's. Hitler's admiration for American race law was actualized in the Nuremberg Laws, which drew on American jurisprudence to define who counted as Jewish.[30] In a kind of geopolitical eugenic synergy, Jews fleeing Nazi Germany's application of eugenic laws were stymied by America's immigration exclusions when the *St. Louis,* a ship carrying nine hundred refugees, was turned away.[31]

The immigration quotas of 1924 were overturned by the Immigration and Nationality Act of 1965. Yet the politics that championed racial exclusion haven't disappeared. Jeff Sessions, who served as President Trump's first attorney general and a longtime Alabama senator, praised the 1924 Immigration Act as model legislation to which the nation should return.[32]

America's major political realignments have also pivoted on the role of race in the polity.[33] Following the Civil War, the period known as Reconstruction saw a flowering of political progress, with Black representatives elected to Southern legislatures, the extension of voting rights to Black men, and the growth of Black political and social organizations. The Thirteenth, Fourteenth, and Fifteenth Amendments to the Constitution were designed to protect Black rights: outlawing slavery, granting birthright citizenship and equal protection of the law, and protecting Black men's suffrage, respectively. W.E.B. Du Bois lauded the period of Reconstruction as a "brief moment in the sun" for Black Americans, and the historian Eric Foner went so far as to call the Reconstruction amendments a "Second Founding" that reshaped the nation by writing Black people's full citizenship into the Constitution.[34] But that moment in the sun was indeed brief, as the shade of Redemption fell across the South in 1877, just twelve years after the end of the Civil War. White Northern and Southern politicians again sacrificed Black social and political rights for white political unity. A bargain over the contested 1876 election handed victory to the Republican Rutherford B. Hayes in exchange for the withdrawal of Northern troops from the occupied South.[35]

Redemption facilitated nearly a century of systematic white supremacist violence. Jim Crow was a system of total social control designed to reinforce Black subjugation through nearly every aspect of daily life. Segregation ensured a ritual obedience reinforced through acts both big and small. Drinking fountains and bathrooms were separated. Courtrooms divided Bibles so white and Black oaths didn't mingle. And to ensure whites' shoes wouldn't step on Black footprints, railroads segregated boarding stairs.[36] Black Americans' constitutional rights were (once again) stripped, often through the selective application of allegedly race-neutral laws such as poll taxes and literacy tests. Black people deviating from these intricate Jim Crow strictures could be murdered, and their killers could be relatively comfortable in their impunity. Vigilante terrorism enforced the elaborate system of social control—night rides, the burning of Black homes and businesses, beatings, and lynchings. This terrorism was sometimes tacitly, and sometimes openly, supported by the state.

Civil rights movement activists challenged the murderous regime of Jim Crow with audacity, bravery, and the moral force of nonviolence. And the activists won, overturning decades of Jim Crow by creatively undermining the logic of white supremacy. Victory was enshrined in the Civil Rights Act, the Fair Housing Act, and the Voting Rights Act, laws that attempted to guarantee rights that were, in some cases, *already granted* by the Reconstruction amendments or prior civil rights acts. That is, white lawmakers had often undermined, ignored, or found elaborate workarounds when white supremacist goals conflicted with the Constitution.

This brief historical sketch isn't meant to be comprehensive. But it should make it clear that racism has been an always-contested feature of American law and policy. Racism was by no means an unfortunate deviation from high-minded ideals, an unfortunate quirk, an aberration, or a mistake. Racism is a basic organizing principle in America's political history and part of a larger system of white supremacy. For much of that history, the upholding of racist ideals was treated by some legal practitioners as obvious, natural, normal, and unbiased. Just as some Americans opposed the abolition of slavery and the Reconstruction amendments' extension of Black rights, others have never stopped fighting against the gains of the civil rights movement. Given the centrality of race to America's founding documents and political history, it is no surprise that ideas about race (and racism) would also shape the subsequent path of American law.

FIGHTING AGAINST RACISM IS *ALSO* CENTRAL
TO AMERICAN HISTORY

America's racial history is not simply a story of domination. At each point along this historical trajectory, Black political thinkers (and their antiracist allies) consistently refused the narcotic mythology of America's racial innocence and steady progress. The historian Robin D. G. Kelley calls the work these thinkers produced "freedom dreams"—a body of emancipatory Black thought that may be America's most authentic political philosophy.[37] These freedom dreamers include writers, poets, abolitionists, and activists who are simultaneously the deepest believers in the possibility of human freedom and the nation's most incisive (and realistic) critics.

Freedom dreams have always felt threatening to the beneficiaries of structural racism. Contemporary attacks on critical race theory are part of a long history that sees antiracist thought generally, and Black American political thought specifically, as dangerous and un-American. Prior to the Civil War, the state of Georgia was so incensed by William Lloyd Garrison's antislavery activism that it offered a bounty for his capture and hoped to put him on trial for his abolitionist agitating. During Jim Crow, anti-lynching activists such as the pioneering journalist Ida B. Wells and the NAACP's executive secretary Walter White risked their lives to report on the brutal ritualized murders of Black

Americans.[38] At the height of the civil rights movement, a coalition of white and Black students protesting segregation, known as Freedom Riders, were firebombed and beaten for audaciously challenging segregation by sitting together on buses. And America's greatest prophet of nonviolence, Dr. Martin Luther King Jr., was repeatedly attacked, arrested, accused of subversion, surveilled, encouraged to commit suicide by the FBI, and ultimately murdered for challenging America's racial divisions.

In each of these cases, opponents of racial equality sought not simply to destroy antiracist messengers but to make understanding and fighting against racism unthinkable. Beyond their activism, Dr. King, Garrison, and Wells developed a written body of antiracist thought that was threatening to white power. Opponents (who apparently feared intellectual honesty) misrepresented Black thinkers and their allies by developing conspiracy theories about their motivations and using the law to silence them (for instance, by arresting Dr. King). Critical race theory builds on the work of these activist-thinkers. And contemporary attacks on critical race theory are updated versions of prior campaigns attempting to silence antiracist thought. The harms attributed to critical race theory (disturbing white children, undermining the nation) are truly astounding (and defy any sense of reality). Critical race theory's opponents have revived the misrepresentations, conspiracies,

and falsehoods used to discredit prior generations of scholars and activists.

Attacks have greeted critical race theory throughout its
history. Whenever powerful people feel the need to refute
the premise that racism is central to American life (typically because current events threaten to confirm that premise), critical race theory jumps from the confines of academic
journals and into the news. For instance, conservatives attempted to paint President Obama as a radical by circulat-
ing a video where he introduced Professor Bell when he
was speaking at Harvard.[39] These attacks are always framed
as a response to the allegedly dangerous ideas put forward
by critical race theory. But in truth, there has never been a
structural explanation of racial inequality that was pleasing
to guardians of the racial status quo.

In her recent book *The Sum of Us,* Heather McGhee argues that the zero-sum battles over race and racism that
have shaped American history hurt white people, too.
McGhee uses the evocative historical metaphor of draining
public swimming pools following the outlawing of segregated public accommodations. Rather than share their
pools with Black Americans, white cities and towns often
chose to close the pools or pave them over. To deny Black
Americans access to leisure and fun, they destroyed their
own leisure and fun, losing public works, spaces to socialize, and places to play.[40] Like a kid who flips the checker-

board when they lose a king, faced with a choice between playing by the rules and sharing, or destroying the game, policy makers have often chosen the latter.

CAVEATS

The people and organizations who weaponized critical race theory are engaged in a very different project than the one you will find in this book. As Adam Serwer has written about the controversy over the 1619 Project (which is often conflated with critical race theory), the debate isn't over facts: the debate is over who has the power to define the past in hopes of shaping the future.[41]

No book of this size could possibly cover the full body of scholarship on critical race theory. In my work, I say I apply "ideas from critical race theory to classic sociological questions." I phrase it this way because critical race theory didn't originate in the social sciences (although, as I show, we sociological race scholars share some intellectual precursors and central ideas), and I am not a legal scholar. This book focuses on empirical research in the social sciences to highlight the key tenets of critical race theory. Each chapter explains a central concept from critical race theory, such as the idea that races are social—not biological—creations (chapter 1), that racism is endemic and structural (chapter 2), and that whiteness is a form of property (chapter 6). I take this approach for two reasons. First, critical race theory started in the law but has been interdisciplinary from the outset, drawing on history and the social sciences. Second, this book is one answer to several requests from critical race theorists such as Kimberlé Crenshaw to expand beyond the law.[42] Scholars such as Devon Carbado and Daria Roithmayr ask for ideas from critical race theory to be measured against social science findings that can allow theorists to confirm, refute, or revise their thinking.[43] This book shows the usefulness of this approach, arguing that critical race theory matters because it provides a better explanation for the resilience of racial inequality than individualist theory describing racism as a negative personal quirk.[44]

Although the scholarship claiming some relation to critical race theory is broad, practitioners have intense disputes over disciplinary, methodological, and epistemological issues. For instance, some think hypotheses derived from critical race theory shouldn't be tested, while others (like myself) think they should.[45] And the continued utility of concepts such as intersectionality and identity politics is debated among academics and the general public. Scholars recognize that knowledge creation is a communal project that proceeds through attempts to resolve these disagreements, in hopes of producing a better shared understanding of the world. Despite these disagreements, critical race theorists recognize that racism is a structural feature of American society, and they share a commitment to racial equality.

ON
CRITICAL
RACE
THEORY

CHAPTER 1

THE SOCIAL CONSTRUCTION OF RACE

The black man is a person who must ride "Jim Crow" in Georgia.

W.E.B. DU BOIS[1]

If men define situations as real, they are real
in their consequences.

WILLIAM I. THOMAS AND DOROTHY S. THOMAS[2]

RACE IS A COLLECTIVE HALLUCINATION

Race is a political and social category, not a biological one. As a political category, the concept of race (falsely) attempts to homogenize and array groups on a hierarchy of superiority and inferiority, variously justified by science, custom, or law. In the language of social science, the shorthand for this categorization and differentiation is that race is a social construction. Seeing race as a social construction turns mainstream ideas about race on their head. Social construction is anti-essentialist, assuming there are no meaningful biological differences between groups, and thus there are no inherent qualities confined to any socially defined racial group. Social construction is a potentially lib-eratory idea that recognizes that all racial groups display the full human range of emotions and intelligence. No group is inherently oppressive or likely to hold a monopoly on truth, beauty, or knowledge.

Rather than an eternal, unchanging, and essential iden-tity, race is contextual, malleable, and unstable.[3] Racial classifications have changed dramatically over the course of U.S. and world history: racial categories vary across soci-eties and between regions within societies. Many individ-uals have even moved from one racial classification to another over their lifetimes. Because racial categories are unstable, law and social policy have repeatedly attempted to pin them down by citing proportions of "blood" or "an-cestry," examining hair texture and skin tone, or even cus-toms and culture.

When confronted with the idea that race is a biological fiction, some conclude race should be abandoned as a way of categorizing people and understanding social inequali-ties.[4] The reasoning behind the urge to abandon race is *su-perficially* compelling (see the THERE IS ONLY ONE RACE, THE HUMAN RACE bumper sticker). If race is a collective halluci-nation (and it is), then why should scholars use it to describe people or differences between groups? If racial categories don't correspond to an underlying essence, then what are they describing?

It's tempting to hope that abandoning race as a descriptive category will lead to a post-racial utopia. But the belief that dropping racial categories will lead to transcending racial inequality relies on a basic misunderstanding of what social construction means. Those who advocate for colorblind approaches often presume that race-based inequalities will magically disappear if social scientists and governments stop cataloging and start ignoring them. But the experience of countries like France, whose republican ideology eschews identity categories ("We are all French") and bans the state collection of data on race, shows that officially ignoring and disregarding racial categories doesn't make inequalities disappear. Despite officially colorblind state policy, France exhibits racial inequality in labor markets and education, and institutionalized discrimination against its Muslim population.[5] Calls to ignore race, in practice, often mean ignoring racial inequality.

Social construction isn't synonymous with "not real." Seeing social constructions as not real, and therefore ignorable, is a common misrepresentation of the terminology (not coincidentally, this misrepresentation often comes from people opposed to interventions that would alleviate racial inequality). People acting on ideas can greatly impact our reality, even if those ideas bear only a dubious connection to truth. For instance, QAnon conspiracy theorists, who believe a gang of Satan-worshipping child-sex traffickers controls U.S. politics and media, have done quite a bit of damage despite their ideas having no correspondence to reality. False ideas inspired an adherent of Pizzagate (a precursor to QAnon) to grab his AR-15 and raid a pizza parlor, hoping to interrupt a nonexistent child-trafficking ring.[6] And false ideas propelled QAnon members' participation in the January 6, 2021, Capitol insurrection, threatening American democracy.[7]

Currency is a good example of how social constructions work to connect communally agreed upon abstractions to substantively important outcomes. Money relies on collective faith in a shared set of beliefs about exchange, value, credit, and legal enforceability. These shared beliefs shape behaviors from working to paying bills. Beliefs about money shape concrete actions, including sanctions should individuals try to avoid agreed-upon commitments. Telling a mortgage lender that you no longer share their faith in the value of this exchange, and are stopping monthly payments, would leave you homeless. Telling a loan shark you don't plan on honoring your financial arrangements might leave you legless. And the collective belief in the value of money helps to coordinate actions globally. The computer I'm typing this on is composed of parts from around the world that were assembled for profit.

Just like the collective belief in currency, shared ideas about race shape social relationships, at scales ranging from our local neighborhoods to the global division of labor. Race is biologically insignificant, but it doesn't follow that it is *socially* insignificant. Race is politically and socially real because, as with currency, people have imbued the concept with a value.

Seeing race as a social construction is different from arguing that there are no phenotypic or genetic differences between people. Rather, social construction means that these superficial phenotypic differences are less important than the social, economic, and political meanings that racial categories have historically been assigned. Critical race theorists have repeatedly shown how laws have discounted phenotype in favor of maximally restrictive racial categories. Collective beliefs about race rely upon (and reinforce) a set of ideas about the relationship between arbitrary physical characteristics, the geographic origins of our ancestors, and the relative worth of human bodies. Once people shape their behaviors around the fake news that race is a biologically meaningful category (or other social constructions) for long enough, these ideas can have real political consequences.

RACIAL CATEGORIES ARE REFLECTIONS OF POWER

The idea that race is a biological reality is a pervasive and powerful myth. Yet genetic, social scientific, and historical evidence all confirm the idea that race is a social construction. Announcing in 2000 the draft results of the Human Genome Project, which sought to map and categorize the full range of human genetic variation, President Bill Clinton said, "One of the great truths to emerge from this triumphant expedition inside the human genome is that in genetic terms, all human beings, regardless of race, are more than 99.9 percent the same."[8] In the decades since the human genome was mapped, scholars have confirmed that population genetics do not support commonsense ideas about biological races.

Even genetic testing companies, whose business model relies on selling a connection to one's forebears, admit their products can't tell people what racial category they belong to, because genetic distributions and socially defined races diverge. Genetic testing companies provide a broad probabilistic—not definitive—estimate of one's ancestry. But genetic ancestry and socially defined racial categories don't always correspond. Racial categories do not map onto the underlying genetic differences between groups typically categorized as "races." If people were divided according to these underlying distributions, the categories would look very different from the racial classifications we use in the United States. For instance, the U.S. census's current racial classification system divides people into six possible racial categories, including "Other." While many people assume the census's racial categories reflect biological differences, the census has changed its classifications repeatedly, adding or subtracting categories in response to social movements or racist panics.[9] According to the present classification system, sub-Saharan Africans and Australian Aborigines are considered Black. But these populations are further apart genetically than any others on earth.[10] Moreover, ancestry testing companies rely upon proprietary algorithms, meaning analyses from different companies sometimes disagree.[11] Even the seemingly objective results of genetic testing are open to interpretation and influenced by preexisting beliefs about one's racial identity. When people receive the results of these genetic tests, respondents sometimes reject findings that don't comport with their aspirational identities.[12]

The commonsense notion of race as a biological category started breaking down in the 1930s and early 1940s, as anthropologists and sociologists increasingly questioned the concept's scientific validity. Challenging the era's eugenics movement, these scholars showed that racial categories were incoherent and scientifically indefensible. Columbia University anthropologist Franz Boas, often considered the founder of modern anthropology, argued that culture, not race, explained differences between groups. Boas and his colleagues challenged scientific racism by showing that researchers were unable to agree on the basic features that supposedly constituted racial groups. These culturalists "delighted in pointing out the discrepancies in between them [racial classifications], showing that scientific racists could not agree on such seemingly simple matters as how many races there were or what criteria—blood, skin color, hair type—best indicated race."[13]

Racial disparities in social outcomes don't imply biological differences. Boas pointed out that eugenic scientists wrongly attributed to biology inequalities that were better explained by unequal social conditions. It is, after all, unsurprising that life expectancy and educational attainment were lower among groups who were systematically denied equal access to healthcare and education by state-sponsored segregation. Eugenicists who attributed differences in life expectancy and literacy rates to biology were laundering social prejudices through scientific jargon, by *providing a defense of* and *justification for* racial inequality, not an explanation of underlying causes.

W.E.B. Du Bois, who saw Boas as an intellectual ally, also argued that race was a fundamentally political relationship. Modern racial classifications were invented, in part, to justify colonialism and slavery. That is, racial categories didn't arise to explain difference; instead, racial categories used arbitrary physical differences to justify exploitation. Structural racism created race. Like Boas, Du Bois explained the conditions of Black people in America by pointing to our history of racial exploitation and exclusion. Du Bois also highlighted the utility of America's absurd racial classification system, arguing that whiteness was a recent political invention grounded in material inequality, whose creators believed they were entitled to global dominion.[14]

America's history of racial categorization can't be separated from its specific form of hereditary slavery. Critical race theorists show that U.S. laws defining racial categories were designed to monopolize the privileges associated with whiteness. Enslavers feared losing a valuable invest-ment: their own enslaved children, who were often con-ceived through sexual assault. If the children of these sexual assaults were classified as white, they would under-mine the institution of racial slavery and the economic in-terests of their enslavers. Prizing money over the familial bond, enslavers created a legal regime ensuring that a child's racial classification followed the mother's. This social classification system incentivized sexual assault and marked enslavers' own children for hereditary, perpetual bondage.[15]

Anxieties surrounding sex, economics, and racial mix-ing didn't disappear after slavery. Following abolition, the United States' one-drop rule of racial classification (also called "hypodescent") was designed to protect the eco-nomic interests that underwrote Jim Crow and assuage fears about passing. According to the sociologist F. James Davis, by 1920 the United States developed a historical in-novation in racial classification, decreeing that one's race didn't automatically follow that of one's mother or father. Any black ancestry made one legally black. The United States remains the only place where racial classifications exhibit the rigidity of hypodescent. For instance, Brazil's racial classification system relies more heavily on skin tone, so siblings who are light- and dark-skinned may get different legal classifications. Under South Africa's apartheid system, nonwhite people who got better educations, had good jobs, or lived in "good" neighborhoods could, on rare occasions, be reclassified as white (the Brazilian colloquialism "Money whitens" captures this dynamic).[16] Even the Nazis, when attempting to define who counted as Jewish under the Nuremberg Laws, rejected the American one-drop model of racial classification as "too extreme."[17]

Critical race theorists show that the many legislative attempts to pin down the elusive factors of "race" make the incoherence of racial categories more apparent. Law has always shaped, and often determined, a person's racial categorization and the rights attendant to category membership. Yet legal classifications of race are no less contrived than scientific ones. During the eugenics movement, fears of miscegenation led states to enact laws barring interracial marriage. Although the one-drop rule of racial classification was a broadly shared consensus across the United States and was repeatedly upheld by courts, many states developed local classification systems.[18] However, these local racial definitions were equally unstable, even as they were being encoded in the law. The incongruity between state classifications led to absurdities. Would crossing state lines mean crossing racial categories if a person with one-eighth Black "blood" entered a state that classified people with one-quarter as Black?[19] Sociologist Michael Omi shows how this incoherence affected Susie Guillory Phipps, who had lived her entire life believing she was white. At forty-three, Phipps discovered that she had been classified by a midwife as "colored" on her birth certificate. Phipps sued to be reclassified but in 1986 the state of Louisiana ruled that her "great-great-great-great" grandmother's enslavement meant Susie was not entitled to whiteness.[20]

If racial categories were natural categories, legislation policing racial boundaries would be unnecessary. From a scientific perspective, the incoherence of racial categories is a weakness, undermining claims about the connection between biology and outcomes. But for political actors, malleable racial categories are a strength, as the boundaries of inclusion and exclusion can expand or contract according to the needs of the powerful. This selective incorporation of racialized groups has happened repeatedly throughout U.S. history, as groups once considered undesirable, such as Irish and Italian Americans, were gradually absorbed into whiteness.[21]

A belief in the biological reality of race has led to some of humanity's greatest tragedies. Eugenic thinkers plied a misunderstanding of genetics and human reproduction into politics and policy, both in the United States and internationally. In the United States, ideas about the innate inferiority of nonwhites and "mentally unfit" whites led to laws and social practices that are now seen as atrocities. Eugenic thinking was used to justify the involuntary sterilization of thousands of Black, Native American, and Puerto Rican women. Forced sterilization was often carried out without informed consent on unsuspecting women, who believed they were receiving routine medical care. These violations were so common that they were described euphemistically as "Mississippi appendectomies."

The legendary Mississippi activist Fannie Lou Hamer's movement into politics was partially galvanized by her sterilization during "what was supposed to be a minor procedure" to remove a tumor. Hamer confronted the doctor who violated her by destroying her ability to have biological children. But she realized attempting to pursue justice as a Black woman in the Jim Crow South would be, as she put it, "screwing tacks into my own casket."[22] From a modest background (her parents were sharecroppers) and without a strong formal education, Hamer nonetheless became a force in national politics, helping with voter drives in the South as a field secretary for the Student Nonviolent Coordinating Committee and establishing the National Women's Political Caucus with Gloria Steinem and Shirley Chisholm. Hamer's experience shows the long reach of eugenic thought, and the power white doctors wielded over Black women in the Jim Crow South.

Despite their name, these so-called Mississippi appendectomies were not restricted to the South. Dorothy Roberts found that up to one-third of women of childbearing age had been sterilized in Puerto Rico by 1968. Sterilization wasn't limited to the island; Roberts quotes a New York

City director of obstetrics and gynecology who claimed, "In most major teaching hospitals in New York City, it is the unwritten policy to do elective hysterectomies on poor black and Puerto Rican women."[23] Science and law—couched in a discourse of detached objectivity—rationalized eugenic sterilization to rob women of color of their reproductive freedom.

Eugenics targeted people of color, but it was also a misguided attempt to "perfect" the white race through breeding. In his book *Imbeciles: The Supreme Court, American Eugenics, and the Sterilization of Carrie Buck*, Adam Cohen uses the case of Carrie Buck to chart the history of eugenic thinking in American law. Carrie was a white foster child of the Dobbs family, but they treated her more as a domestic than a daughter. After the Dobbses' nephew sexually assaulted Carrie, the family blamed her, and the state placed the child that resulted from the assault with the Dobbs family. To cover up the crime and protect their reputation, the Dobbses had Carrie committed as "feebleminded" (although this accusation was untrue). Once she had been committed, the state of Virginia claimed that Buck's mother and child were also mentally unfit and moved to have Buck sterilized. Buck fought for her reproductive rights, but the Supreme Court ruled her sterilization constitutional, and the liberal justice Oliver Wendell Holmes justified the destruction of reproductive rights with the infamous quote "Three generations of imbeciles are enough." American eugenic policy, based on the belief that race is a biologically meaningful category, also had international implications. Cohen claims that "Nazis who had carried out 375,000 forced eugenic sterilizations cited *Buck v. Bell* in defense of their actions."[24]

The notion that race is a biologically meaningful category is based upon a set of demonstrably false ideas about human bodies—that racial groups are discrete and knowable, that they are relatively unchanging, and that a natural hierarchy exists. This false line of reasoning has justified the taking of land, the theft of labor, state-sponsored segregation into under-resourced neighborhoods and reservations, and genocide. For critical race theorists, social construction means the attention given to physical differences is less important than the political uses for which physical differences provide a convenient excuse. The mythology of biologically meaningful racial differences serves not as a valid explanation for inequality but as an alibi for crimes in progress.

CHAPTER 2

STRUCTURAL RACISM

Racism is like a Cadillac, they bring out a new model every year.

MALCOLM X[1]

What white Americans have never fully understood—but what the Negro can never forget—is that white society is deeply implicated in the ghetto. White institutions created it, white institutions maintain it, and white society condones it.

THE NATIONAL ADVISORY COMMISSION ON CIVIL DISORDERS
(KERNER COMMISSION REPORT)[2]

RACISM IS COMMON, ROUTINE, AND ORDINARY

Critical race theorists see racism as common, routine, and ordinary, not rare, aberrant, or unlikely. Typical definitions of racism see it as a special category of meanness. In this view, racism is perpetuated by bad, prejudiced individuals who hold negative ideas about a racial out-group. These negative ideas or stereotypes are seen as stable personal attitudes that, when acted upon, are discriminatory. Under mainstream definitions, racist figures are easy to recognize. They are police with their murderous knees on Black men's necks, Civil Rights–era cops straining against dogs trying to maul peaceful protesters, or torch-bearing Klansmen. Racism is thought of as primarily interpersonal, implying that once individuals are held accountable for racist incidents, the problem is solved. Educate these backward figures, and racial enlightenment awaits. Critical race theorists call this mainstream definition of racism the "perpetrator perspective," because it evaluates racism based upon individual culprits' intent.[3]

Rather than seeing racism as purely individual, critical race theorists argue that racism is structural. Structural racism recognizes that discriminatory ideas are important, especially when those ideas are combined with access to resources that allow for the creation of resilient systems of inequality. Structural racism can be perpetuated through conscious intent, unconscious bias, or policies and practices that privilege one racial group over another. Structural racism creates harm through the control of legitimate social organizations—including the court system, police departments, schools, banks, hospitals, and real estate offices—on a scale that far surpasses isolated individual meanness. Control of these organizations connects individual discriminatory actions to larger patterns. Structural racism doesn't mean individual racism is inconsequential. It means individual racism is empowered by its incorporation into a system that can magnify its impact through biased patterns of resource allocation. Discriminatory police officers are backed by state power, and discriminatory employers are rarely held legally accountable.[4] When biased processes are built into policy rules or the law—such as exams for college entry or policing that requires racial profiling—structural racism compels even people without individual animus to participate.

Defining racism from the perspective of perpetrators—rather than as a political system that distributes resources unequally—is advantageous for the beneficiaries of that system. Seeing racism as a negative personal quirk obscures how individual acts of discrimination can pass benefits to entire communities. A white homeowner who refuses to sell to a Black family, thereby keeping the neighborhood mostly white, reinforces residential segregation and contributes to the value of all the houses in a neighborhood.[5] The ripple effects of housing discrimination don't stop at individuals, as property taxes fund schooling and contribute to the nation's vast educational disparities. Opportunities are downstream from education, so racial inequalities built into schooling cascade across one's life. Privileging the perspective and internal feelings of individual racists also allows people who vicariously benefit from discrimination to believe that, because they haven't used a racial slur or denied anyone a loan, they are unimplicated and untouched by the wider system of structural racism. Seeing education alone as the solution to racism ignores the fact that many of the most sophisticated manifestations of racism—from eugenics to mass incarceration and immigration restrictions—were developed and implemented by the most educated people in American society.[6] Perhaps most important, seeing racism as a negative individual quirk makes it difficult to understand the depth and resilience of racial inequality.

STRUCTURAL RACISM IS A POLITICAL SYSTEM

Critical race theory thus replaces the perpetrator perspective with an understanding of structural racism as a political system. Calling racism political doesn't mean it is partisan (throughout much of U.S. history, white supremacy was a bipartisan project), although partisans can and do use racist appeals to garner support. Structural racism is political in the sense that it helps to determine differential access to employment, healthcare, education, and other important resources. As a political system, racism may be *reflected* in individual actions and attitudes, but it isn't *reducible* to those actions and attitudes.[7] Structural racism is a distributional system that combines ideas about race with unequal access to social and material resources.[8]

Structural racism's conceptual roots are found in *Black Power: The Politics of Liberation* by Student Nonviolent Coordinating Committee chairman Kwame Ture (formerly known as Stokely Carmichael) and political scientist Charles Hamilton, first published in 1967. The first chapter of that book discusses institutional racism:

When White terrorists bomb a Black church and kill five Black children, that is an act of individual racism, widely deplored by most segments of the society. But when in that same city—Birmingham, Alabama—five hundred Black babies die each year because of the lack of power, food, shelter and medical facilities, and thousands more are destroyed and maimed physically, emotionally and intellectually because of conditions of poverty and discrimination in the Black community, that is a function of institutional racism. . . . But it is institutional racism that keeps Black people locked in dilapidated slum tenements, subject to the daily prey of exploitative slumlords, merchants, loan sharks and discriminatory real estate agents. The society either pretends it does not know of this latter situation, or is in fact incapable of doing anything meaningful about it.[9]

The problems Ture and Hamilton highlighted in 1967 are still here. Although the concept of structural racism emerged from social movements to explain the unjust system they were protesting, the concept is widely accepted among scholars. Nearly every indicator of social well-being—health,[10] income, wealth,[11] life expectancy, and occupational standing—shows that white people are, on average, doing better than people of color in general, and Black people in particular.

Structural racism is powerful because once discrimination is built into a system, and that system comes to be seen as legitimate, commonsense, or "just the way things are," it obscures the roots of inequality. For instance, many don't know the history of collusion between banks and federal and local governments that created residential redlining that locked people of color in under-resourced neighborhoods, or how housing discrimination contributed to contemporary racial wealth gaps.[12] Lacking knowledge around the causes of racial inequality makes it easy for people to assume that it results from some deficiency with the culture or work ethic of people of color, rather than a planned, expected, and predictable result of social policy.

Segregation is the basic unit of structural racism because segregation facilitates resource hoarding. Informal discussions often refer to "segregated" schools or neighborhoods as synonyms for under-resourced Black and Brown communities. But this elides the fact that white neighborhoods and schools are also segregated spaces.[13] All-white or nearly-all-white spaces aren't accidental; they are the intended outcome of exclusionary policies and practices.[14] Instead of being named as such, however, segregated white spaces are often described with seemingly race-neutral terms such as "good" neighborhoods and schools. The "good" parks, schools, grocery stores, and other amenities that are overrepresented in white areas are resources protected and hoarded through processes of segregation.

Structural racism reflected in segregation means communities of color are less likely to live near a hospital, less likely to have access to healthy choices around food and exercise, and less likely to have access to a high-quality education.

EVIDENCE OF STRUCTURAL RACISM IS COMPELLING AND OVERWHELMING

The stakes of individual racism are changing people's feelings. The stakes of structural racism are, fundamentally, life and death. Ruth Wilson Gilmore defines racism as "the state-sanctioned or extralegal production and exploitation of group-differentiated vulnerability to premature death," tying the consequences of systematically under-resourcing nonwhite communities to dire outcomes.[15] In isolation, a negative attitude is relatively inconsequential. But when people are empowered—as bosses, teachers, or doctors—to channel their negative attitudes into the denial of resources, including access to competent and equal medical care, it can steal time, in the form of life expectancy, from people of color.[16]

Ture and Hamilton's visceral description of Black babies dying in Birmingham highlights that structural racism in America begins taking a toll before birth. Preexisting conditions and unequal treatment in the healthcare system mean Black women are more than twice as likely to experience stillbirth.[17] The Black infant mortality rate is 2.3 times higher than that of white infants.[18] Black children are more likely to be born with low birth weight, predisposing them to subsequent illnesses, including heart disease, diabetes, and high blood pressure.[19] Socioeconomic differences don't fully account for these facts, because Black Americans are more likely to die an early death at every education level, and life expectancy gaps between Black and white Americans *are greater* at higher levels of education.[20] Many structural factors contribute to these early deaths for Black Americans. Residential segregation ensures Black Americans are more likely to be exposed to harmful environmental pollutants that can shave years off lives. The daily frictions of racism, from workplace slights to surveillance in stores and neighborhoods, to fighting to have doctors take symptoms seriously, contribute to these adverse health outcomes and early deaths.

Critical race theorists have shown that far from being the answer to racial inequality, America's educational system is a key site in the reproduction of structural racism.[21] At every stage of schooling—from preschool to college—Black and white students experience the educational system differently. Nearly three-quarters of a century after the landmark *Brown v. Board of Education* decision outlawing state-sponsored segregation, the American system of schools remains separate and unequal.[22] The U.S. elementary school system is highly segregated, and after declines until the

1980s, some schools are resegregating.[23] Black and Latino children often attend schools with high levels of impoverished peers.[24] Recall that schools serving students of color are relatively under-resourced because U.S. schools are funded in part by a property tax system whose values are indexed to residential segregation. The vast wealth disparities created through decades of state-sponsored segregation impact per-pupil spending, with students of color receiving less on average.

Within schools, Black preschool-aged boys are twice as likely to be expelled compared to their white and Latino counterparts.[25] Black girls, who make up just 20 percent of female preschool enrollees, account for "54 percent of girls receiving one or more out-of-school suspensions."[26] Some are quick to attribute these differences to behavior, but research shows that identical behaviors typical of all children—like interrupting a teacher—are interpreted differently based on students' race, with Black students punished more harshly than white students.[27] As students move through middle and high school, Black children are more likely to be tracked into noncollege pathways. Tracking within schools can create the kind of segregated education that used to be accomplished by separate buildings for white and Black children.[28]

Educational inequalities between Black and white students are often used by conservatives and moderate liberals to claim there is some problem with Black students. Black students are said to lack a work ethic or have cultural problems ("They accuse high achievers of 'acting white'") that predispose them to educational underachievement. But the so-called "acting white" hypothesis has repeatedly been knocked down by research consistently showing that Black students are *more likely* to say they value education than white students.[29] Surveys show Black and Latino parents are more likely to say a college degree is essential for their children's success than white parents.[30] Black students also overestimate the economic returns they will receive from education because for each level of education they receive, Black people earn less than equally qualified white counterparts.[31] Many school procedures, from test scores to disparate discipline rates to tracking, are presented as neutral evaluations of student behavior and ability. But bias shapes these measures, channeling students into a segregated set of subsequent opportunities for the rest of their lives. Yet, like eugenic theories of prior eras, the acting white hypothesis is like a zombie that won't stay dead.

Structural racism is a basic feature of the American economy. The Black unemployment rate has been twice that of whites for almost fifty years.[32] As Dara Strolovitch points out, the "normal" Black unemployment rate would constitute an economic crisis if whites were experiencing similar levels of economic dislocation.[33] Once a job is secured, employers are more likely to give Black employees variable schedules, making it more difficult for them to plan nonwork time.[34] Even the labor market signal of going to an Ivy League school can't overcome labor market discrimination, as Black Ivy League graduates are called back for jobs at a rate similar to that for whites who attended state flagships. If Black Ivy League applicants are called back, they are offered less prestigious positions with lower salaries.[35] Complaining to human resources about discriminatory treatments is unlikely to help, as Black employees who report workplace bias (or even outright interpersonal racism) often say the response from programs putatively designed to help is worse than the initial discrimination.[36]

Employment discrimination remains common, despite the 1964 Civil Rights Act ostensibly banning the practice. Social scientists often test for racial discrimination through field experiments called "audit studies." Audit studies take equally qualified people from different racial groups, train them to behave similarly (for instance, answering interview questions with indistinguishable prepared responses or using identical résumés), and match them on measures such as attractiveness and educational level. These studies minimize (or eliminate) nonracial factors as explanations for unequal treatment.[37] Once matched on factors that could bias the results, testers venture forth to apply for jobs or loans, buy cars,[38] attempt to rent apartments, or buy a house or get good seats at restaurants.[39] Depressingly, audit studies frequently find that discrimination against people of color remains a widespread feature of American life. The studies also reveal discrimination is often hidden from its victims, who are unaware that racism played a role in their being denied an opportunity.[40]

Results from audit studies can be dramatic because they show how supposedly neutral evaluation processes ("We hire the best candidates, regardless of race") consistently devalue people of color. The Harvard sociologist Devah Pager created a variation on audit studies to see how prison time impacted one's chance of being hired. She found that white men who had served time for a nonviolent drug offense were more likely to be called back for an entry-level job than Black men without a criminal record.[41] In addition, employers who, when surveyed, stated they supported hiring nonviolent offenders fell short of their stated convictions. Self-reporting openness to a post-incarceration second chance didn't translate into a job offer, as those who indicated they would hire an ex-offender were no more likely to do so than survey respondents indicating past incarceration was a non-starter. People are often unaware of their racial biases and therefore discriminate, even when confident that they won't.[42]

Exclusion from opportunities extends far beyond entry-level jobs and in-person audits: even a Black-sounding name is enough to trigger discrimination. Economists Marianne Bertrand and Sendhil Mullainathan scoured major newspapers' want ads and sent nearly five thousand résumés in response. The résumés varied only in the Black- or white-sounding names of the fake applicant (for example, Lakisha or Jamal vs. Emily or Greg). Despite identical qualifications, the Black-sounding names were 50 percent less likely to be called back, showing that racial discrimination in hiring exists "across occupation, industry, and employer size."[43] Evidence from these studies implies that the invisible hand of the labor market is white. What matters in these cases is not just the dislike potential employers have toward people of color. What matters is that they *are empowered by their role as gatekeepers responsible for distributing resources.*

I could go on. The scale, intensity, and historical continuity of racial disparities make individual explanations fall flat. Reducing racism to interpersonal dislike, simple prejudice, or grievance makes it difficult to explain the stunning resilience of racial inequality. Receiving unearned benefits under the relational system of structural discrimination undermines the notion that hard work and merit are the best predictors of economic mobility.[44] And in each of the above cases, the beneficiaries of an unequal system, who likely had no idea that discrimination was happening, may have profited nonetheless.

Structural racism, when built into policies and procedures, obscures the processes that keep racial hierarchies in place. If an entrance exam is racially biased, a teacher who is a committed antiracist, yet grades the exam accurately, will reinforce racial inequality. If a judge harbors no prejudice toward anyone she sentences, but racially biased laws (such as the different penalties for possession of crack or powder cocaine) or patterns of policing (racial profiling) disproportionately send Black or Latino suspects to court, her compelled reliance on mandatory minimum sentencing laws will produce racially disparate outcomes. Rules and laws are designed to shape behavior, especially when individuals would behave differently absent the rule. Once biases are built into seemingly legitimate social sorting mechanisms, no ill intent is needed—following the rules reproduces racial inequality.[45]

Although it is uncomfortable to discuss this, people of color who have been incorporated into biased systems— such as policing—can end up reinforcing structural racism by simply doing their job, as biased policies, laws, and practices compel behavior. Take a hypothetical Black police officer in New York City, where the city's stop-and-frisk policy disproportionately targeted Black and Latino men for police stops (despite police finding more contraband on the white men they stopped). The hypothetical Black officer simply following orders and carrying out this policy is, by doing their job well, contributing to structural racism. Similarly, a Black Supreme Court justice who supports weakened voting rights is helping to institutionalize racism. Biased systems produce biased outcomes, regardless of the identity of the system's administrators.

Structural racism, as both an abstract concept and a set of social practices that are often intentionally obscured, can be difficult to discern. Processes that reinforce structural racism are often neutral seeming and considered legitimate, normal, and "just the way things are." The mundanity of structural racism makes it insidious and hard to challenge. Yet many who deny the reality of structural racism (mostly because it doesn't negatively impact them) recognize how structures work when their tax rate increases, the terms of interest on a loan change, their job benefits are cut, or their kid's school district lines are redrawn. Seeing racism as structural doesn't absolve individuals of complicity in harmful systems. It explains how those systems compel behavior (rules, laws, custom, and tradition), why racism is so resilient (it distributes resources), and why racism impacts so many social domains, from segregated living spaces to disproportionate encounters with police and even life expectancy.

CHAPTER 3

COLORBLIND RACISM

[President Nixon] emphasized that you have to face the fact that
the whole problem is really the Blacks. The key is to devise a
system that recognizes this while not appearing to.

H. R. HALDEMAN, CHIEF OF STAFF TO PRESIDENT NIXON[1]

Some of my best friends are Black.

WHITE CULTURAL APHORISM

Colorblind racism uses allegedly neutral language and policy
toward racially biased ends. Critical race theorists are met
with incredulity when they claim that racism can be invoked
by neutral speech and enacted through race-neutral policy.
Yet hiding intent may be more effective than parading in a
Klan robe, and racially unequal outcomes can be accomplished without an open commitment to white supremacy.

But don't take my word for it; here is Lee Atwater, Ronald Reagan's advisor, making the strategy plain:

You start out in 1954 by saying, "Nigger, nigger, nigger." By 1968 you can't say "nigger"—that hurts you, backfires. So you say stuff like, uh, forced busing, states' rights, and all that stuff, and you're getting so abstract. Now, you're talking about cutting taxes, and all these things you're talking about are totally economic things and a byproduct of them is, blacks get hurt worse than whites. . . . "We want to cut this," is much more abstract than even the busing thing, uh, and a hell of a lot more abstract than "Nigger, nigger."[2]

Atwater wasn't alone in using colorblind racism as a political strategy. Here is John Ehrlichman, a top advisor to the Nixon administration and a Watergate coconspirator, explaining the political calculus behind Republicans starting the so-called "war on drugs":

The Nixon campaign in 1968, and the Nixon White House after that, had two enemies: the antiwar left and black people. You understand what I'm saying? We knew we couldn't make it illegal to be either against the war or black, but by getting the public to associate the hippies with marijuana and blacks with heroin, and then criminalizing both heavily, we could disrupt those communities. We could arrest their leaders, raid their homes, break up their meetings, and vilify them night after night on the evening news. Did we know we were lying about the drugs? Of course we did.[3]

These jarring and deeply cynical quotes explain how political operatives weaponized coded racial appeals. By beginning with ideas connected to white resistance to racial equality (states' rights and forced busing) and slowly increasing the level of abstraction, proponents of this strategy associated seemingly unrelated concepts (taxes or healthcare) with the project of racial subordination ("Blacks get hurt worse"). Atwater also clarifies that the stakes of colorblind racism were partially economic: enhancing whites' relative material position by harming Black people. The colorblind strategy of targeting political enemies without alienating white voters who saw open racism as a taboo helped win elections.

Colorblind racism is characteristic of many of the most damaging rollbacks of civil rights law. By co-opting civil rights language, reactionaries attempted to seize the moral high ground while undermining affirmative action, voting rights, equal employment opportunities, and school desegregation. To take one example, when invalidating a school desegregation plan in *Parents Involved in Community Schools v. Seattle,* Chief Justice John Roberts claimed, "The way to stop discrimination on the basis of race is to stop discriminating on the basis of race."[4] Roberts's superficial (and tautological) commitment to principles of antidiscrimination is belied by the fact that the court's decision in *Parents Involved* nullified a voluntary integration plan. Noting the

use of colorblind language to accomplish color-coded outcomes, critical race theorist Patricia Williams said that the
case "represents, for all intents and purposes, the overturning of *Brown v. Board of Education*."[5]

The strategy of using coded racist appeals has done an
enormous amount of damage by providing an alibi to those
who know that stating their openly racist motives will undermine their goals. But as Ehrlichman and Atwater admit,
America's history of structural racism has encoded unequal
racial processes in many seemingly neutral provisions—
from taxes paid by Black families who were denied access
to the public services their funds paid for, to school districts
whose race-neutral boundaries are drawn around segregated neighborhoods.[6] Because racial meanings are built
into these colorblind processes, talking about taxes and
schools can inspire racial resentment if it implies that "undeserving" people of color are receiving unearned benefits.

Colorblind language is an ideological shield for structural racism, entrenching racial inequality through laws,
policies, and practices that are race neutral in name only.
For example, so-called "broken windows" policing, which
advocated a law enforcement focus on minor offenses
(open containers, putting one's feet on a subway seat), was
a race-neutral policy whose implementation overwhelmingly criminalized young men of color. James Q. Wilson
and George L. Kelling, authors of a classic article advocat-

ing for broken windows policing, recognized that their race-neutral policy could, in practice, promote racial profiling and the violation of basic rights. They wrote:

> We might agree that certain behavior makes one person more undesirable than another but how do we ensure that age or skin color or national origin or harmless mannerisms will not also become the basis for distinguishing the undesirable from the desirable? How do we ensure, in short, that the police do not become the agents of neighborhood bigotry?
>
> We can offer no wholly satisfactory answer to this important question.[7]

Wilson and Kelling couldn't answer the critical question of how racial bias might warp their proposed policy, but nonetheless decided the potential benefits outweighed the costs. This officially colorblind policy had disastrous results for the Black and Latino men whose constitutional rights were routinely violated by police who saw them as suspects.[8]

Colorblind racism shapes the criminal justice system beyond street-level stops, through the system of mass incarceration that disproportionately impacts Black Americans. The scale of American mass incarceration is hard to fathom, with the United States incarcerating more of its citizens than any other nation—including countries considered authoritarian, such as China and Iran. Racial inequalities shape every stage of the criminal justice system, from arrests and convictions to the ability to find work upon release. Mass incarceration has created a system of social control so racially unequal that civil rights lawyer and author Michelle Alexander calls it a "New Jim Crow" that permanently locks the formerly incarcerated out of opportunities.[9] Even though white and Black people use drugs at similar rates, colorblind drug laws championed by politicians across the political spectrum—by design—fell hardest on Black people. These laws, coupled with colorblind over-policing disproportionately targeting Black communities, contributed to the catastrophe of mass incarceration. Colorblind invocations of "law and order" are still a dog whistle, drawing on a history of conflating Blackness and criminality that stretches back to the Reconstruction era.[10]

By using officially neutral (but discriminatory) processes, colorblind racism builds biased practices into the "normal" functioning of America's racial system. By explaining racial inequality as the result of supposedly nonracial processes, colorblind language helps paper over the cognitive dissonance of living in a society whose formal commitment to equal opportunity is belied by the fact of staggering racial inequality. Neutral-sounding language provides plausible deniability for practices that are anything but neutral. Critical race theorists and race scholars generally have shown how colorblind racism shapes politics,[11] neighborhood choices,[12] the criminal justice system,[13] schooling,[14] and many other areas of life where people want to avoid the facts of structural racism.

Colorblind appeals also allow their users to claim their *opponents are bringing race into otherwise race-neutral situations.* Highlighting the codes, dog whistles, and evasions of colorblindness can bring accusations of "pulling the race card," which equates *noticing* racial inequality with *perpetuating* racial inequality. Colorblind racism effectively denies that structural racism is a political system while using racist appeals to gain political power. Nationalist calls to "Make America Great Again," which evince a nostalgia for America's history of open racial domination (when, exactly, were things great for Black folks?), are nonetheless facially neutral. The appeal of these dog whistles lies in their ability to signal intent to like-minded insiders while providing the (admittedly threadbare) sheen of racial innocence. Colorblind rhetoric invokes the zero-sum logic of racism, which treats anything gained by people of color as necessarily taken from white people.[15] And colorblind racism is a political strategy that promises whites they can recover these perceived losses.

THE HISTORICAL ROOTS OF COLORBLIND RACISM

Ehrlichman's and Atwater's colorblind appeals were part of a post–Civil Rights era political backlash called the Southern Strategy, which mobilized racial grievance to recruit disaffected whites to the Republican Party. As Ian Haney López makes clear, "Southern" is something of a misnomer, as the strategy was a national attempt to create a white coalition that transcended class divisions and to force a political realignment in opposition to the civil rights movement. Like Atwater and Ehrlichman bragging about using covert racism, Kevin Phillips—a political prodigy credited as a primary force behind the Southern Strategy—was open about using covert racist appeals to court white voters who were unhappy with cultural change and felt constrained by new racial norms.[16] Civil rights successes made the open use of slurs taboo, so political operatives found a rhetorical workaround.

Presidents Nixon and Reagan heeded their advisors and heartily embraced the Southern Strategy. Both politicians recognized that by the 1970s, the George Wallace playbook of blocking the entrance to the University of Alabama to keep it all white, or yelling "segregation forever," would draw political condemnation. So, stoking fears of continued political unrest from Black protest, Nixon made the plausibly deniable "law and order" and antibusing dog whistles central to his effective presidential campaign. Reagan emphasized "states' rights"—a racist code Atwater highlighted—when launching his 1980 campaign in a speech staged in Neshoba County, Mississippi, where the civil rights martyrs James Chaney, Michael Schwerner, and

Andrew Goodman had been murdered and buried in an earthen dam. States' rights have often been invoked by white southern political actors hoping to stop federal enforcement of the constitutional protections extended to Black Americans by the Reconstruction amendments. The Southern Strategy helped create and solidify the contemporary overwhelming white support for today's Republican Party, which has become a party of white grievance.[17]

Using racially coded language to amass political support is a bipartisan affair that capitalized on real contradictions in the post–Civil Rights era's race relations. Although the Republicans were the political innovators of colorblind racism, Democrats were credible imitators. Bill Clinton borrowed directly from Nixon's language, running as a "tough on crime" "law and order" candidate, who "vowed that he would never permit any Republican to be perceived as tougher on crime than he."[18] Clinton also championed his plan to "end welfare as we know it." Clinton's law-and-order stance drew upon long-standing associations of Black people with criminality. And Clinton's welfare reform policy built upon the thinly veiled gendered racism of Reagan's so-called "welfare queens," which stigmatized public benefits by caricaturing a Black woman for alleged fraud.

Atwater and Ehrlichman updated a strategy as old as the republic. The Constitution avoided using the word "slavery" despite apportioning congressional representation partially based upon the enslaved population. Even the debate over the three-fifths compromise included color-blind elements, gesturing toward principled opposition to slavery based upon universal rights, while ultimately up-holding the peculiar institution.[19] When formal equality was written into the Constitution, Southern white suprem-acists evaded the Fourteenth Amendment by employing facially neutral disenfranchisement practices. Poll taxes and literacy tests were often officially applicable to every-one. In practice, these policies targeted Black people, who were disproportionately in poverty (and thus unable to pay) and less likely to be literate. Local functionaries also em-ployed discretion, unfairly evaluating (or simply throwing out) Black people's tests. Nonetheless, courts often rejected challenges to these disenfranchising tactics, accepting their architects' paper-thin claims of race neutrality. Poll taxes and literacy tests were formally neutral procedures, but any honest observer understood their intent and function. Logical consistency requires the same recognition when contemporary facially neutral practices such as voter ID laws intentionally target Black people.[20]

RACISM WITHOUT RACISTS

Partisan political battles haven't defined the boundaries of colorblind racism: it infects everyday speech. Dog whistles like "thugs," "good schools," and "safe neighborhoods," or phrases like "if *those people* would just work harder" are a linguistic escape hatch for folks who want to say nasty things about people of color without seeming brutish.

Some see colorblind language as unambiguous racial progress. It is good that racial slurs are no longer acceptable in mixed company, and that using racist language may cause legal or professional repercussions. I understand why some view colorblind language as progress, and obviously workplaces and public life should be free of harassment and contemptuous racial slurs. At the same time, by creating evasive language and ready-made alibis, colorblind racism can be difficult to counter. The point of plausible deniability is, after all, denial. By obscuring motives, dodging responsibility, and muddying what "counts" as racism, colorblind language helps to derail substantive changes focused on the material roots of structural racism.

The sociologist Eduardo Bonilla-Silva (who, full disclosure, was one of my graduate advisors) has done more than anyone else to show how colorblind racism helps people explain away racial inequality. Bonilla-Silva recognized that the expression and impact of racism are historically specific and might change in reaction to social pressures. Just as politicians did with their Southern Strategy, regular Americans recognized that association with explicit racism carried a potential social cost. Hoping to show how racial attitudes changed over time, social scientists were still using survey questions designed to measure racism prior to the civil rights movement, which asked questions about neighborhood segregation and interracial marriage. Surveys appeared to be trending toward racial acceptance. But Bonilla-Silva argued that the use of old questions might be misrepresenting abstract rhetorical commitments to equality as racial progress. Social desirability bias—a well-known process where respondents give socially acceptable answers—might mean surveys were picking up symbolic, rather than substantive, advances. Survey research consistently shows that white Americans overwhelmingly claim to support integrated schools, integrated neighborhoods, and intermarriage. Yet communities remain segregated, marriages remain mostly intra-racial, and schools remain largely separate and unequal.

Bonilla-Silva's research highlights the gap between word and deed on race matters, explaining the contradiction between expressed commitments to equality and white Americans' highly segregated daily lives. To get beyond the limits of surveys designed to capture the racial attitudes of a prior era, Bonilla-Silva's interview methodology allowed white Americans to discuss racial matters frankly, beyond the constraints of forced-choice survey questions. These interviews revealed that white Americans' support for racial equality was often conditional. Respondents worried about the children of interracial relationships ("Won't they be rejected by both sides?") and questioned the stability of interracial unions. Respondents worried that neighborhood integration would harm them ("What about our property values?") and expressed concern about the alleged perils of integrated schooling ("But what about our children's safety?"). In his typically pithy fashion, Bonilla-Silva calls colorblindness "racism without racists" in his book with this title.[21] Bonilla-Silva shows that although no one wants the social repercussions that come from being called a racist (even if these repercussions are mostly overstated), few are willing to give up the benefits that come from racialized opportunity hoarding.

Bonilla-Silva holds that four central "frames" organize colorblind racism into a semi-coherent ideology—abstract liberalism, naturalization, the minimization of racism, and cultural racism. Abstract liberalism uses a commitment to equality in principle to avoid supporting policies that would lead to equality in practice. Abstract liberalism sees attention to race itself as the problem and refuses a distinction between policies designed to enforce racial inequality (voter ID laws) and policies designed to alleviate racial inequality (affirmative action).

Naturalization sees unequal outcomes as resulting from supposedly nonracial processes. For instance, claiming segregation is the consequence of "birds of a feather" choosing to segregate housing or dating pools. But there is nothing natural about our highly segregated system that used law and social policy to concentrate Black people in the worst neighborhoods with the least resources. Similarly, a whole host of laws were designed to prevent people from dating or marrying across the color line.

Racism is minimized when the well-documented barriers people of color face are considered immaterial. Hard work and "bootstraps" narratives allow people to ignore labor market discrimination and the economic predation on Black consumers who have often been failed by legal protections.

Cultural racism replaced biological explanations for racial inequality with the idea that black culture is deviant. The many waves of panic over Black styles ("If they would just pull up their pants!" "Hip-hop causes crime!") are examples of cultural racism. Cultural excuses for racial inequality aren't applied evenly, as extremely violent white movies and music are held to lower standards, rarely invoked as explanations for white violence. And cultural explanations ignore the fact that civil rights martyrs like Dr. King weren't saved by dressing well.

Together, the frames of colorblind racism provide people with a rigid yet situationally adaptable set of explanations justifying contemporary racial hierarchies in ways that sound race neutral. Colorblind racism allows people to have "principled" opposition to policies that are designed to intervene in historical harms such as affirmative action or reparations while ignoring the contemporary impact of generations of policies intended to subjugate people of color.

Colorblind policy became a constitutional imperative at the very moment race-conscious policy was being used to, ever so slightly, even the playing field. Thurgood Marshall, in his dissent to the *Regents of the University of California v. Bakke* case, pointed out the nonsense of colorblind approaches to solving racial inequality. The *Bakke* decision recognized that universities had a compelling interest in using race to diversify their student bodies but outlawed the use of race to ameliorate the harms of slavery, Jim Crow, or ongoing discrimination. Marshall wrote, "During most of the past 200 years, the Constitution as interpreted by this Court did not prohibit the most ingenious and pervasive forms of discrimination against the Negro. Now, when a state acts to remedy the effects of that legacy of discrimination, I cannot believe that this same Constitution stands as a barrier."[22] Colorblind racism worked to stifle Black advancement by equating ameliorative and regressive race policy.

Contemporary defenders of colorblindness often cynically misrepresent a quote from Dr. King's "I Have a Dream" speech from the March on Washington to bolster colorblind policies. Hoping for a day when his children would be "judged by the content of their character, not the color of their skin," Dr. King realized that America's centuries of structural racism meant that ameliorative, race-conscious policies were necessary to achieve substantive equality.[23] Elsewhere, Dr. King wrote, "A society that has done something special to harm the negro should now do something special to help him."[24] Putting aside the craven appropriation of Dr. King's words by politicians who would have opposed him in life, and who promote policies that undermine his legacy, attributing colorblindness to Dr. King may be the apotheosis of the colorblind strategy, as it uses his words in opposition to his goals of substantive racial equality. Misrepresenting Dr. King's quote on the color of one's skin says a lot about the content of one's character.

Structural racism means substantive racial inequality will proceed through inertia, without intervention. And colorblind racism justifies racial inequalities by smoothing over the contradictions between the nation's purported devotion to equal opportunity and the reality of deep, lasting, and seemingly intractable racial disparities. Just as policy makers don't attempt to solve poverty by ignoring unemployment, wages, and taxes, racialized social problems won't be solved through colorblindness. People who claim they are colorblind or "don't see race" are making a willful decision to avoid seeing how race is used to distribute privilege and peril.

CHAPTER 4

RACIAL PROGRESS

> If you stick a knife in my back nine inches and pull it out six inches, there's no progress. If you pull it all the way out, that's not progress. The progress is healing the wound that the blow made. They haven't even begun to pull the knife out, much less heal the wound. They won't even admit the knife is there.

MALCOLM X[1]

> Black success beckons the mob.

DR. KORITHA MITCHELL[2]

THE ALLURING MYTHOLOGY OF INEVITABLE PROGRESS

America's standard narrative of racial progress has all the reductive trappings of a fairy tale. On one side lurks the ominous evil of white supremacy (an evil that, Voldemort-like, many analysts fear to name). The founders were great, if flawed, men, who declared their independence with the claim that "all men are created equal." But this rarely named evil ensnared those founders in what Republican senator Tom Cotton calls the "necessary evil" of slavery (of course, necessary *for whom* is left unsaid).[3] On the other side, there are a few reluctant heroes: a weary Rosa Parks refusing to give up her seat; Dr. King marching to fulfill his dream; and the hope, change, and progress that propelled Obama's unlikely presidential campaign. In the storybook version, these plucky heroes' efforts eventually win out, solving racism. The moral of this fairy tale is straightforward. Racial issues are always (and inexorably) improving, with the nation moving toward a "more perfect union." The extension of rights to formerly excluded racial and ethnic minorities is viewed retrospectively as inevitable, and rights gained are seen as permanent. Contemporary inequality is residual from an earlier, less enlightened time. Perhaps most important, there is nothing to complain about. People of color should be grateful things have come so far: they should stop kneeling and behave.

Like most effective propaganda, America's reigning narrative of racial progress takes partial truths and attempts to elevate them to incontestable facts. Ending the institutionalized terrorism of Jim Crow and the victories of the civil rights movement undoubtedly opened opportunities to people of color. Prior to the civil rights movement, discrimination was open, legal, and routine. Following the civil rights movement, discrimination is covert, illegal (but rarely enforced), and routine. The mainstream narrative of racial progress also downplays the violent resistance civil rights activists faced, and that resistance to integration and equal opportunity had never really ended.

PROGRESS IS FRAGILE AND REVERSIBLE

Critical race theorists reject the mythology of racial progress. Things are not always getting better. One measure of racial progress is this just-so story moving from slavery, through Jim Crow, to the real but incomplete victories of the civil rights movement. A different measure of progress is the space between the two seconds it took police to shoot Tamir Rice[4] for playing with a toy gun in a park in 2014 and the four seconds it took police to shoot Atatiana Koquice Jefferson[5] while she was playing video games at home in 2019. For those at the bottom of America's racial hierarchy, progress has always been contingent, contested, and revocable.

In place of the progress fairy tale, critical race theorists draw on the extensive history of American racism to argue that progress is not linear but fitful—full of challenges, entrenched opposition, and in some cases, outright reversals. Derrick Bell summed up the conflict and changing historical fortunes that characterize America's relationship to racial progress:

> Black people will never gain full equality in this country. Even those herculean efforts we hail as successful will produce no more than temporary "peaks of progress," short-lived victories that slide into irrelevance as

racial patterns adapt in ways that maintain white dominance.[6]

Bell recognized that no single law or policy will permanently eliminate racism. Challenging the notion of linear racial progress, Bell pointed out that opponents of racial equality have been quite creative in developing new strategies of racial exclusion. Like a game of whack-a-mole or the heads of a hydra, when one form of discrimination is outlawed, new forms often arise to take its place.[7] The U.S. racial order may be more remarkable for its profound continuity than the moments of radical social change following the Civil War and the civil rights movement. As Michelle Alexander claims, "We have not eliminated racial caste in America; we have merely redesigned it."[8]

Voter suppression laws show how new methods of racial exclusion can arise in changed historical circumstances. In 2013, the Supreme Court eviscerated Section Five of the 1965 Voting Rights Act in *Shelby County v. Holder*. Section Five required states with a history of discrimination to get federal approval of proposed changes to voting procedures. Since the court's decision in *Shelby*, new methods of stealing, undermining, or complicating the voting rights of people of color have exploded. Resurrecting tactics from Jim Crow, Republican legislators have promoted or implemented voter ID laws, roll purges, attempts to restrict voting hours or relocate polling places, and outright voter intimidation.[9] Following the 2020 election, and former president Trump's lies about voter fraud, these democracy-undermining tactics of racial disenfranchisement have gone into overdrive, with normally staid commentators pointing out that they threaten not just the voting rights of people of color but American democracy.

The Voting Rights Act was a crowning achievement of the civil rights movement, the result of decades of Black and allied organizing, in conditions that were often deadly. Given that all rights in a democracy are protected by the franchise, eroding the ability of people of color to vote endangers everything from antidiscrimination laws to being protected from physical violence. That the nation needed the 1965 Voting Rights Act was itself a nod to the fragility of racial progress. The Voting Rights Act simply outlawed the many voting impediments Southern states adopted following the Reconstruction amendments, which theoretically offered equal protection of the law, including the franchise.[10] If progress was secure once obtained, the Voting Rights Act would have been redundant.

When cutting the heart out of the Voting Rights Act, Chief Justice Roberts relied upon the woefully inadequate fairy-tale conception of progress. The Voting Rights Act substantially increased Black turnout, in part because pre-clearance procedures ensured that states with a history of voter discrimination couldn't create new mechanisms of

disenfranchisement. To justify removing preclearance procedures, the court's majority noted these Black voting
gains. But not as evidence that the policy was working as
intended and should be left in place. Rather, Chief Justice
Roberts claimed, "Our country has changed," implying that
hard-won voting rights wouldn't be erased if voting protections were removed.[11] The reasoning in *Shelby* didn't consider that the districts subject to preclearance were
reporting less discrimination precisely because these re-
quirements effectively kept them from discriminating. In
her dissent, Justice Ruth Bader Ginsburg pointed out the
majority's backward logic, writing, "Throwing out pre-
clearance when it has worked and is continuing to work to
stop discriminatory changes is like throwing away your
umbrella in a rainstorm because you are not getting wet."[12]
Declines in voter suppression didn't result from changing
hearts and minds but from altering the structure of voting
law. With *Shelby*, the court essentially used a mistaken notion of progress to argue that voting protections, and the
racial progress they promoted, had gone far enough and
should go no further.

White Americans have often reversed progress when
feeling threatened by the economic success of people of
color. Before the Black rebellions of the 1960s, "race riots"
were popularly understood as white violence against Black
and other communities of color, often in response to economic competition.[13] The 1921 Tulsa, Oklahoma, massacre,

where approximately three hundred Black people were murdered and thousands displaced from its "Black Wall Street," was only one of at least thirty-two, and possibly more, such attacks on Black communities. Threatened by a prosperous Black enclave (and believing economically secure Black people were acting above their station), white mobs, often joined by law enforcement, used simply incredible levels of violence to destroy Black progress. These attacks included dropping aerial bombs in Tulsa and the National Guard turning machine guns on the Black community in Knoxville, Tennessee. Like lynching, these brutal attacks were often pretextual, designed to terrorize entire communities and rationalized by false allegations of assaults on white womanhood. And terrorize they did, destroying wealth and influencing residential patterns to this day as Black families were displaced and their property was stolen. The routine destruction of Black property, wealth, and lives to stop racial progress was rarely investigated or seen as warranting federal study and intervention.[14]

Racial progress can also quickly be wiped out without physical violence. The "last hired, first fired" pattern of employment during economic downturns routinely results in Black people facing greater precariousness for longer periods of time. The Great Recession, whose causes are partially located in banks targeting Black communities for subprime loans,[15] created the "greatest loss of assets in history for Black and brown people."[16] Of course, banks like Wells Fargo were able to target Black communities for sub-prime loans in the first place because of the nation's overall lack of progress on lessening residential segregation. Health gains, too, are fragile, because of how America routinely shifts risks onto Black workers. The coronavirus pandemic reversed ten years of progress on closing the life expectancy gap between Black and white Americans.[17]

White Americans' belief in substantial racial progress even alters their ability to accurately comprehend contemporary inequality. Writing in *The Atlantic,* the Yale social psychologist Jennifer Richeson outlines a series of studies that she, Michael Kraus, and their collaborators conducted to show how notions of progress shape white perceptions of the racial wealth gap. When asked how wealth inequality has changed between the years 1963 and 2016, white Americans consistently, and significantly, overestimate Black American wealth at every point in time. For instance, white Americans assume that in 1963 Black people held 50 percent of the average wealth of white Americans, when their share of wealth was only 5 percent. Remarkably, respondents' understanding of the size of the racial wealth gap showed greater inaccuracy as they moved toward the present, indicating their belief in substantial progress. In a second study, whites were divided into two groups and asked a series of questions about racial progress. During this study, one group was told the magnitude of the contemporary wealth gap before being asked questions about the historical size of the disparity. The respondents who received accurate information were more likely to describe present-day wealth distribution as unequal. But rather than accepting the fact that time has not greatly lessened the racial wealth gap, they revised their understanding of the historical gap, imagining the past as more unequal rather than revising their belief in substantial progress. For white Americans determined to believe racial inequality is receding, the empirical reality of contemporary inequality can't displace the fairy tale of progress.[18]

Derrick Bell's observations on the fickle nature of racial progress led him to claim structural racism was "an integral, permanent, and indestructible component" of American life, constantly reasserting itself through new policies or laws when old methods of oppression were foreclosed.[19] Opponents of Bell's paint this notion that racism is permanent as unnecessarily pessimistic, pitting Bell against the supposedly sunnier prescriptions of thinkers like Dr. King. Often misrepresented as having a singular focus on American progress ("The arc of the moral universe is long, but it bends towards justice"), Dr. King's views were much more complex. While locked in a Birmingham jail for protesting the city's stubborn and brutal resistance to integration, Dr. King critiqued the idea that progress was natural or inevitable. He warned against:

the strangely irrational notion that there is something in the very flow of time that will inevitably cure all ills. Actually, time is neutral. It can be used either destructively or constructively. I am coming to feel that the people of ill will have used time much more effectively than the people of good will.[20]

Dr. King's views on racial progress were tempered by the reality of massive white resistance—in the North and South—to the civil rights movement. Many white Americans thought the movement had gone too far, disapproved of the tactics of nonviolent civil disobedience, or thought the extension and enforcement of constitutional rights for Black Americans was happening too fast.[21] Dr. King summarized these paternalistic requests for patience by noting that claims of slow, steady progress were often cover for stagnation. King wrote, " 'Wait' has almost always meant 'Never.' . . . We have waited for more than three hundred and forty years for our constitutional and God-given rights."[22]

Expecting optimism about progress from people who were systematically denied constitutional protections for three hundred and forty years (and whose rights have often been tentatively enforced since) is strange, morally and intellectually. Morally, asking for optimism in the face of ongoing structural racism decenters the reality of racial oppression in favor of assuaging the conscience of people

unwilling to deal with (or supporting) that reality. Intellectually, expecting optimism ignores history and the experience of current inequalities in everything from education
to income to access to voting. Bell's caution against a too-
sunny picture of progress wasn't despairing. Like Dr. King,
Bell was careful not to place a nebulous hope for future
equality ahead of the concrete political steps necessary to
achieve such a future. And like Dr. King, Bell saw the
struggle for racial equality itself as redemptive, despite the
odds. He wrote, "The fight in itself has meaning and should
give us hope for the future."[23] Throughout American history, Black people have never been treated as full, equal
citizens. Stating this isn't pessimism but simple fact. Assuming the continuity of structural racism is more realistic
than the perpetual promise that equality is imminent.

Change and progress aren't necessarily synonyms.
Forms of racial domination have changed dramatically over
time—from slavery and Jim Crow to mass incarceration,
from overt economic exclusion to covert discrimination—
but the United States' racial hierarchy has consistently
placed Black Americans at or near the bottom. Many of the
contemporary changes in the racial order, such as the coordinated attack on voting rights, are part of a backlash to
perceived progress. Like the definition of individual racism
outlined earlier (chapter 2), the fairy tale of racial progress
remains compelling for some because it is politically useful
and deeply flattering to white Americans who don't want

to feel implicated. Seeing the worst kinds of racism as safely quarantined in the past absolves people of contemporary actions, like sending their kids to segregated schools, that reinforce racial inequality. The progress fairy tale also plays upon the notion that America is a uniquely exceptional nation whose flaws are self-correcting (e.g., that the "original sin" of slavery created the avenue for a racial redemption), that structural racism is a slight deviation from America's destiny, and that the nation has corrected course. The trope of progress is used to make current movements for racial equality, such as Black Lives Matter, seem ungrateful and illegitimate for refusing to recognize the benevolence—and essential goodness—that led to social change. Racial subjugation is not a sidenote in American history. Racial subjugation is an ongoing project where many mainstream institutions continue to discriminate against people of color. Narratives of inevitable progress downplay this history of racial oppression, making contemporary domination difficult to understand and challenge.

CHAPTER 5

INTEREST CONVERGENCE

In light of the sorry history of discrimination and its devastating
impact on the lives of Negroes, bringing the Negro into the
mainstream of American life should be a state interest of the
highest order. To fail to do so is to ensure that America
will forever remain a divided society.

THURGOOD MARSHALL[1]

THE SPACE TRADERS

Aliens want America's Black people. Arriving from a distant star in freighters the size of aircraft carriers and speaking through the stupefying voice of President Reagan, the aliens offer a trade. Hand over everyone legally classified as Black and, in return, they will erase America's national debt, restore the environment, and provide limitless clean energy.

The America where the aliens arrive is led by a fake-populist president who sees this intergalactic ethnic cleansing as a political lifeline. Shipping Black people to space would free his party from the economic and environmental consequences of their leadership. An interracial coalition resists the trade, including business leaders who fear a loss of profits (from both increased labor costs when they can no longer underpay Black people and decreased income when they can no longer overcharge Black people for goods). But after an intense national debate (as is often the case when majorities vote on minorities' fate), white Americans decide that the trade is worthwhile. In a scene recalling the sadism of the Middle Passage and chattel slavery, Black Americans are rounded up, stripped, herded onto freighters, and sent into space.

This alien abduction, from Derrick Bell's short story "The Space Traders," draws on history to make the case that the "space trade" isn't a one-off proposition.[2] Stability, rather than progress, is characteristic of America's racial order, and the wager of Black life for white gain is ongoing. Bell's parable is designed to illustrate his theory of interest convergence, which claims "the interest of blacks in achieving racial equality will be accommodated only when it converges with the interests of whites."[3] When the aliens arrived, interests diverged, and Black lives were sacrificed for white progress.

THE GEOPOLITICS OF CONVERGING INTERESTS

Bell focuses on the landmark *Brown v. Board of Education* decision to make his case that interest convergence, rather than benevolence or morality, explains periods of racial progress. It may seem quixotic to choose *Brown*, a case that is usually considered a crowning achievement of the civil rights movement and is widely accepted (at least rhetorically) across the political spectrum. *Brown* has an undeniable moral force that partially arose from the drama of the famous Dolls Test conducted by the psychologists Kenneth and Mamie Clark. Black children were presented with dolls and asked, among other questions, to choose if white or Black dolls were "nice" or if they preferred one over the other. Two-thirds of the Black children chose the white doll, which the researchers and the court took as evidence of the psychological injury imposed upon innocent Black kids by the stigma of racial segregation.[4] The court cited these results to support the claim that state-sponsored segregation harms Black children by imparting "a feeling of inferiority as to their status in the community that may affect their hearts and minds in a way unlikely ever to be undone."[5] Segregation applied a permanent badge of subjugation.

The victory in *Brown* was the result of a decades-long movement demanding greater access to educational resources and the push for equal schools that occupied generations of activists. Across these decades, the immorality of racial segregation was always clear. The immorality was the point, as segregation ensured Black children's futures were hobbled, making it difficult for them to compete. Yet for decades courts were unmoved by this injustice, repeatedly affirming the farce of "separate but equal" despite clear evidence that Black schools in the South were woefully, insultingly, and intentionally unequal. And the decades of activism hadn't pushed public opinion in the white South toward desegregation. Jim Crow—like contemporary structural racism—was seen by many beneficiaries as a natural system that, if not ordained by God, at least resulted from some deficit in Black people. Following *Brown,* opposition to segregation led to a set of ingenious racist strategies of "massive resistance" to avoid integrating or to reimpose segregated schooling. These schemes, which were coordinated attempts to subvert the law, included opening private "segregation academies," white flight from integrating areas, and homeschooling. In Virginia, white parents were so opposed to integration that they closed the public schools for five years, denying their own kids access to public education rather than allowing them to learn alongside Black children.[6]

Surveying the landscape of white resistance to desegregation, Bell argues that *Brown* wasn't the result of a great moral awakening on the part of the Supreme Court or the broader white polity. Bell contends, "The decision in *Brown* to break with the Court's long-held position on these issues cannot be understood without some consideration of the decision's value to whites."[7] Bell found the source of *Brown*'s value to white Americans in a heightened geopolitical position. Proxy states were susceptible to Soviet Cold War propaganda that capitalized on the United States' state-sponsored discrimination. Black WWII veterans, connecting American racism to the international condemnation of Nazi atrocities, refused to accept the Jim Crow order to which they were returning. And like slavery in the nineteenth century, Jim Crow racial etiquette was becoming a barrier to further Southern economic development.[8]

Cold warriors, vying for influence in decolonizing proxy states, knew Soviet propaganda that capitalized on racism was effective and potentially embarrassed the nation's leaders by showcasing American hypocrisy globally. It was in white America's interest to show that the nation could deal with the problem of racism. Analyzing U.S. State Department and Department of Justice files, the historian Mary Dudziak later showed that Bell's analysis was correct. With America's global standing at risk because of its treatment of Black Americans, white American policy makers were willing to formally call for desegregation.[9] Progress, when it has come for Black Americans, has typically come with equal or greater benefits for white Americans.

Bell acknowledges, in both "The Space Traders" and his writing on *Brown*, that white American opinion is not uniform. There have always been white Americans deeply committed to racial equality, "for whom recognition of the racial equality principle was sufficient motivation" for outlawing school segregation and opposing racism generally.[10]

Bell nonetheless argues that absent interest convergence, when the equal protection clause of the Fourteenth Amendment comes into conflict with the social standing of middle- and upper-class white Americans, the courts are likely to sacrifice abstract principles of equal treatment to these Americans' interests. Of course, deviations from principle will be couched in neutral-sounding language that is often violated by racial reality.

Bell's story uses a fictional alien invasion to highlight the calculus of trades that powerful white people have often made and the dystopian conditions these trades impose upon Black Americans. Some white Americans are deeply offended by "The Space Traders" and the broader idea of interest convergence. In 2012, "The Space Traders" became one of the many cudgels, like the Reverend Jeremiah Wright and birtherism, that opponents swung in the hopes of bludgeoning President Obama's ambition. Obama had introduced Bell when he was a student at Harvard Law School. Conservative pundits used this brief association, and "The Space Traders," to claim that Obama was a radical, and decried Bell's work as inflammatory and unrealistic.[11]

I can see readers balking at the idea that white Americans would happily, or even grudgingly, trade Black life for large or even small gains. "The Space Traders" challenges the mythology of racial progress, which claims we have learned from the mistakes of our unfortunate racial past and moved on. Interest convergence calls into question the notion of the essential innocence of the broader polity and the notion that racialized elements of public policy are a deviation, rather than a norm.

But the response to the coronavirus pandemic should shake, if not entirely overturn, the idea that some Americans wouldn't make Bell's trade when interests diverge. In the first year of the coronavirus pandemic, Elizabeth Wrigley-Field, a sociologist at the University of Minnesota, compared white people's excess mortality from the pandemic to a "normal" year's mortality rate for Black Americans. She found that if the worst pandemic since the 1918 flu killed only white people, whites' total death toll would still be less than the deaths Black Americans experience during a normal year.[12] Structural racism, expressed through the stresses of dealing with discrimination, differential exposure to harms, inferior schooling, and substandard healthcare, regularly shortens Black life. And the United States accepts, almost without question, pandemic-scale Black death every year.

Some individual-level responses to the pandemic also indicated a willingness to shift risks onto nonwhites. As armed white men stormed state capitols to protest pandemic lockdowns, and white women threw tantrums about mask tyranny, the price that Dr. Bell's invaders offer—environmental restoration, freedom from debt, and limitless clean energy—seemed an overestimation. White folks protesting for their right to infect were willing to weigh the lives of disproportionately Black and Brown workers against their desire for a manicure, a haircut, a cup of coffee, or a tattoo.[13]

Even before the pandemic, in his book *Dying of Whiteness: How the Politics of Racial Resentment Is Killing America's Heartland,* the psychiatrist Jonathan Metzl showed that many white Americans were willing to support policies that risked their own health as long as nonwhites were hurt worse. According to Metzl, racial resentment has led many white Americans to repeatedly vote against their self-interest, supporting policies that make them sicker and lead to earlier death, such as opposing universal healthcare if it is rhetorically associated with a Black president. For instance, Tennessee's refusal to expand Medicaid "potentially cost every single adult Black and white resident of the state somewhere between two and five weeks of life."[14] White citizens were unwilling to see their hard-earned tax dollars spent on people they considered to be unworthy (minorities who "don't pay their fair share" and immigrants). Refusing to see that their interests were tied up with those of their fellow Black and Brown citizens, white voters supported policies that harmed their own families and communities. Not coincidentally, Tennessee has passed an anti–critical race theory law that allows funding to be withheld from public schools that teach so-called "divisive concepts," which would presumably include facts about racial animus and the denial of healthcare.[15]

Interest convergence recognizes that politics is a game of compromises. Democracies assume that competing coalitions vying for resources will sometimes win outright victory, sometimes reach an impasse, and sometimes compromise. Although recent years have seen a sharp increase in asymmetrical polarization, with the right wing moving well outside post-1965 norms of political agreement— including the legitimacy of elections and democracy itself— there is a long history of believing compromise is the way out of political impasses. Interest convergence acknowledges one such compromise: America's history of white bipartisanship was built upon agreement that Black rights were mostly optional. As the Harvard political scientists Steven Levitsky and Daniel Ziblatt argue in their book *How Democracies Die,* the periods of greatest bipartisan agreement in the United States happened during eras when Black rights were explicitly suppressed. America has been a functioning multiracial democracy only since the passage of the 1965 Voting Rights Act. Prior to that, the American political system was, at best, selectively democratic.[16] Interest convergence lays bare the fact that minority group rights are revocable, subject to the majority's whims.

Bell writes elsewhere that many Black folks accepted the basic soundness of "The Space Traders" and weren't at all shocked by the implication that their fellow citizens might trade their rights for riches.[17] And Bell doesn't delve into the psychology behind whites' acceptance of the trade but claims some white Americans don't see racial equality as legitimate.[18] A deeply ingrained sense of white superiority makes equal outcomes seem suspect. That is, racial *inequality* is an expected norm, and narrowing income or education gaps are often taken to mean something has gone wrong and should be remedied. Scholars of race and ethnicity have long maintained that racial inequality may serve as a baseline against which whites measure their relative standing.[19] A century ago, W.E.B. Du Bois argued that some white people interpret statistical evidence of Black suffering not with horror, but as a signal that their position is secure.[20] Du Bois claimed, "To the millions of my people no misfortune could happen,—of death and pestilence, failure and defeat—that would not make the hearts of millions of their fellows beat with fierce, vindictive joy."[21] White joy at Black misfortune was premised on the relative protection whiteness granted. Crises inflicted on Black Americans weren't seen as disastrous but rather as a confirmation for many white Americans that things are as they should be, a reflection of the natural order.

White Americans have, with important exceptions, accepted the profound racial inequalities of our society because it typically means they are slightly less exposed to risks than they would be otherwise. Policies that could revoke the trade, or at least make its terms less stark, such as reparations or even universal healthcare, are often rejected on the grounds that they would subsidize undeserving minorities. Even a state's relative generosity of welfare benefits, whose beneficiaries are majority white, decreases as minority population rises.[22]

Bell's aliens have always been here. It is only a slight exaggeration (and a fair one at that) to say that the history of American public policy can be told as a series of trades on the value of Black life.

CHAPTER 6

WHITENESS AS PROPERTY

Whiteness is the ownership of the earth forever and ever, Amen!

W.E.B. DU BOIS[1]

For much of U.S. history, whiteness meant one could legally enslave people, and their children, in perpetuity—and whiteness protected one from being so enslaved. Whiteness meant that supposedly binding treaties were mere suggestions. The state could usurp the land of Native Americans and hand that stolen property to white settlers. Whiteness allowed people to eliminate economic competition through the mob violence of lynching, or through riots destroying Black communities, and face no legal consequences. Whiteness granted the franchise, freeing its bearers from the despotism imposed upon people of color whose voting rights were denied. Whiteness provided poor whites the psychological balm of knowing that despite poverty, their social station would remain above the wealthiest Black person. Whiteness still makes it easier to avoid unwarranted harassment from the state, to accumulate wealth, to get a job or rent an apartment, and to live a relatively long and healthy life. Whiteness, like race generally, is a social construction, and the root of that construction is differential access to resources. Whiteness is *property*.

Seeing whiteness as property isn't hyperbolic: it is an accurate description of a fundamental set of social relations that still shape American life. In her classic *Harvard Law Review* article "Whiteness as Property," Cheryl Harris shows that whiteness is not (just) a racial identity; it is a possession built upon the exclusion and exploitation of people of color.[2] America's history of racialized slavery and the theft and redistribution of native land created a tether between racial identity, economics, and property rights. Theorists such as James Madison argued that property should be thought of expansively, as "all of a person's rights." America's legal delineation of racial categories—by design—truncated the property rights of nonwhite groups. When the Supreme Court decided the 1857 *Dred Scott* case, it made this clear, claiming those classified as Black had "no rights a white man must respect."[3] Although the historical connection between whiteness and property has been weakened by broad movements for racial justice, this progress is often precarious, subject to changing political and even contextual whims. White racial identity (or even the "prox-imity" to whiteness as manifest through skin tone and pass-ing), or the ability to navigate white cultural norms by "code-switching" in schools and workplaces, continues to tie whiteness to property and privilege.[4]

Harris draws on stories—both personal and political—to show how whiteness and property are fused. Harris's grandmother was a Mississippi sharecropper who joined the vast flow of millions fleeing the mundane, normalized terrorism of Jim Crow. Harris's grandmother landed in a highly segregated Chicago and discovered that, as Malcolm X claimed, the U.S. South began at the Canadian border. Chicago's racial etiquette differed from Mississippi's. But North or South, whiteness shaped access to job and hous-ing opportunities. Although she was legally classified as Black, outside the context of her birth, Chicago's relative anonymity presented Harris's grandmother with a devil's bargain: continue to experience the economic deprivation she fled Mississippi to escape, or temporarily pass as white and gain access to the property she was arbitrarily denied. Harris's grandmother chose the latter, commuting across the highly segregated city to work in a department store. Passing provided the capital of whiteness and access to work. But passing was psychologically taxing. Temporarily shedding an identity, denying family, and working in an all-white space—where anti-Blackness may be so ambient that it is taken for granted—took an emotional toll. Harris's description of her grandmother's disgust at passing is visceral and moving. Her co-workers' open racism, and the denial of her identity, created psychological scars that were evident to Harris decades later.

Harris's grandmother's decision to pass as white can't be separated from political definitions of whiteness that courts used to curtail (or facilitate) access to property. Passing, and the ambiguity around access to resources that such race-shifting entails, were central to the 1896 U.S. Supreme Court case *Plessy v. Ferguson*. This case made the self-contradicting phrase "separate but equal" law, ushering in decades of legal segregation in American life. *Plessy* revolved around Louisiana's 1890 Separate Car Act, which mandated segregation on trains. Homer Plessy was chosen as the test case for challenging segregation laws because his ability to pass as white—so activists thought—would highlight the fundamental absurdity of segregation laws. In delineating Plessy's ancestry as "seven-eighths Caucasian and one-eighth African blood," the court claimed his Blackness was phenotypically "not-discernible."[5] Plessy's lawyer argued that this non-discernible Black background entitled Plessy to the same rights as a white man. But in a political system that parceled out rights according to racial categories, physical imperceptibility was no bar to legal definitions of race.

Plessy bought a first-class ticket and sat in the whites-only section of the train, informing the conductor, who was a coconspirator in the challenge to segregation, that he was "colored." After "learning" of Plessy's racial classification, the conductor ordered Plessy to move to the Black car. Plessy refused, precipitating his arrest and subsequent test of segregation ordinances in the courts. Despite the "imperceptibility" of his legally assigned race, the Supreme Court ruled that racial lines had to be drawn somewhere. Protecting the property of whiteness, they chose the invisible traits of Plessy's ancestry.[6] Although *Plessy* and *Dred Scott* were testing distinct legal questions in very different eras, the court in both cases agreed on the principle that Black folks had "no rights a white man must respect."[7] *Plessy* did include a vigorous dissent, from Justice John Harlan, which famously argued that "our constitution is colorblind." But Harlan made an exception to his own argument, claiming that Chinese people were so alien to (white) Americans that they could be barred from citizenship.[8] Passing, as did Harris's grandmother, or choosing not to pass, as in Plessy's case, shows how whiteness can dictate access to (or the denial of) property rights.

THE WAGES OF WHITENESS

The property interest in whiteness brought psychological peace of mind to poor whites. Following the Civil War, the relatively elevated social position that poor whites had enjoyed compared to the enslaved was challenged. Newly freed people with marketable skills were now potential labor competition. Emancipated Black laborers, should they join a labor movement with poor white workers, could also have wrenched concessions from Southern capitalists rebuilding the war-ravaged economy. According to W.E.B. Du Bois, Southern political leaders interrupted this potential interracial class alliance by playing on the white prejudice nurtured by centuries of racial enslavement. Segregation and the associated subjugation rituals legalized by *Plessy* were constant reminders to whites of their legally elevated social position. W.E.B. Du Bois called the sense of superiority imparted by the Jim Crow racial etiquette a "public and psychological wage" that was tied to material reality through segregation. The separation between Black and white determined differential access to nearly every resource:

> They were given public deference and titles of courtesy because they were white. They were admitted freely with all classes of white people to public functions, public parks, and the best schools. The police were drawn from their ranks, and the courts, dependent upon their votes, treated them with such leniency as to encourage lawlessness. Their vote selected public officials, and while this had small effect upon the economic situation, it had great effect upon their personal treatment and the deference shown them. White schoolhouses were the

best in the community, and conspicuously placed, and they cost anywhere from twice to ten times as much per capita as the colored schools. The newspapers specialized on news that flattered the poor whites and almost utterly ignored the Negro except in crime and ridicule.[9]

People make sense of their place in the world by comparison with similar others, and external reference groups shape people's relative sense of status. White Americans were provided access to jobs, housing, schools, and full participation in public amenities with other white people across class status. What Du Bois called the "wages of whiteness" helped to forge a white intra-racial alliance, undermining class-based solidarity with Black people in favor of a race-based sense of community. Choosing race-based solidarity over class had real consequences for poor whites, whose decision to exclude Black Americans from unions likely depressed their own wages.

Dividends from the wages of whiteness are still being collected. The mid-twentieth-century rise of the middle class was fueled by access to debt that allowed whites to accrue wealth.[10] Historians and social scientists have exhaustively documented how facially neutral, supposedly "universal" programs have contributed to the property interest in whiteness. In his classic *When Affirmative Action Was White: An Untold History of Racial Inequality in Twentieth-*

Century America, the historian and political scientist Ira Katznelson chronicles the many ways federal policy transferred resources to whites, providing property that people of color were denied.

Black people were systematically excluded from the twentieth century's sweeping, transformative social programs responsible for creating the white middle class. Southern legislators, uncomfortable with progressive economic policies that might undermine the white supremacist order, had extracted concessions for their votes. Protections extended to white workers excluded domestic and agricultural laborers—occupations with a disproportionately nonwhite pool of workers. This exclusion denied Black workers the basic tools, such as collective bargaining, that led to concrete economic gains for white workers.[11]

When outright exclusion wasn't written into the GI Bill, Southern legislators ensured that supposedly universal programs were administered by discriminatory local functionaries. Black WWII veterans, who fought fascist racial ideology in segregated units, returned home to be denied the GI Bill benefits they had earned through their service. Black veterans were stripped of their education benefits through a segregated higher education system that wouldn't accommodate the numbers of Black veterans seeking entry, or were outright denied federally backed loans. The specifics on the extent of inequality in the distribution of GI Bill benefits were staggering. According to the Duke economist Sandy Darity and the independent scholar A. Kirsten Mullen, in 1947 only two Black Mississippi veterans received a home, business, or farm loan out of the 3,229 loans disbursed. They continue, "At no other time in American history has so much money and so many resources been put at the service of the generation completing education, entering the work force, and forming families. Comparatively little of this largesse was available to black veterans. With these policies, the Gordian Knot binding race to class tightened."[12]

Twentieth-century social policies such as the New Deal and the GI Bill are clear cases of whiteness serving as a kind of property that could generate future economic returns. The fusion of whiteness and property through social policy shapes contemporary wealth inequality, and the wealth gap between Black and white families has *increased* in recent decades. Thus, the profound contemporary wealth gap can be partially traced to years of government-sponsored racially unequal access to home loans, and to redlining policies that have led to slower appreciation rates in nonwhite areas, even though redlining is now banned. Following patterns of median wealth inequality over twenty-five years (1984–2009), Thomas Shapiro and colleagues show the wealth gap between white and Black families "nearly triples, increasing from $85,000 in 1984 to $236,500 in 2009," at the height of the Great Recession.[13] Wealth differences don't imply white families have Bill

Gates or Elon Musk money. Historic and contemporary discrimination mean white families are more likely to have a nest egg, or the ability to help their kids with a car or home down payment. Wealth disparities make it more difficult for Black families to weather downturns, job loss, or other economic crises. And wealth can make the difference between oppressive and merely inconvenient student debt.[14]

Harris's original discussion of whiteness as property focused on the access to employment that passing as white provided her grandmother. Contemporary critical race theorists have built upon this idea to show how downplaying one's racial identity can facilitate acceptance from white gatekeepers.[15] Recognizing that race is a complex social construction, the sociologist Ted Thornhill conducted an experiment showing how admissions counselors screen Black applicants according to the salience of their racial identity. He sent emails to 517 white admissions counselors pretending to be a potential Black applicant. Some of these fake prospective students claimed they were involved in racial justice education and politics. Another group presented themselves as unlikely to participate in racial politics, preferring "neutral" (or white) sounding extracurriculars. Thornhill found that white admissions counselors were more likely to reply to students who were not involved in racially salient political activities.[16] Downplaying the salience of one's racial identity can also lead to concrete benefits when Black employees code-switch, by eschewing

Black vernacular and styles in workplace interactions (and likely making their white colleagues more comfortable). But, as was the case for Harris's grandmother, who was racked by the costs of downplaying her racial identity for economic gain, code-switching impacts Black employees' psychological well-being and contributes to the sense that they don't belong in the workplace.

Conceptualizing whiteness as a form of property reframes wealth accumulation, notions of merit, so-called "neutral" employment standards, and the long shadow of historical discrimination. Structural racism is a material relationship, and the preconditions of contemporary wealth disparities are found in racially biased government policy and law. Many white families have indeed worked hard and sacrificed. But Black families were often legally locked out of the wealth-generating mechanisms white families accepted as their birthright. Racial inequality arose not out of a superior white work ethic but from aspects of structural racism that transmuted whiteness into property.

CHAPTER 7

COUNTERNARRATIVES

For the native, objectivity is always directed against him.

FRANTZ FANON[1]

I stood at the border, stood at the edge and claimed it as central.
I claimed it as central and let the rest of the world move
over to where I was.

TONI MORRISON[2]

The video was clear. Walter Scott was running away with his back turned, posing no threat. Officer Michael Slager fired eight times. Five of those shots hit Walter Scott, killing him. After murdering Scott, Officer Slager walked toward and dropped a taser next to Scott's body, in an apparent bid to plant evidence that would justify murder.[3]

The video of Derek Chauvin kneeling on George Floyd's neck was also clear. Like Walter Scott, Floyd posed no threat, as he was handcuffed on the ground and not resisting when Chauvin applied his body weight to Floyd's neck for nine minutes, choking Floyd to death.[4]

Despite the clarity of the videos, in both cases the police

reports were opaque narratives designed to absolve mur-
derers. In Scott's case, Officer Slager claimed that he "feared
for his life because the man had taken his stun gun," even
though Scott was fleeing when Slager gunned him down.
In Floyd's case, the Minneapolis Police Department released a misleading account of Floyd's murder. They
claimed Floyd was in "medical distress" but omitted that
Officer Chauvin's knee was likely the cause of that deadly
distress. The media, in both cases, initially reported the
claims of the police officers, reinforcing their narrative of
innocence. Facts in these cases came to light because of by-
standers' videos—not because of police trustworthiness or
reporters' doggedness. Prosecutors or juries who relied
solely on police narratives would have been misled, and a
semblance of justice denied to the dead.

Black Americans have long had counterstories to official
police narratives, arising from generations of differential
treatment. Some Black families prepare their sons for interactions with the police (a practice common enough that it
is known colloquially as "the talk"). A somber rite, the talk
instructs Black boys to perform deference ("move slowly,"
"comply") in the hope that said rituals can minimize the
likelihood of being brutalized by the police.[5] Decades of
polling data show that Black Americans have less trust in
the police and believe that police use disproportionate
force against people of color.[6]

Prior to the kinds of video evidence made possible by

the ubiquity of cellphone cameras, Black people's accurate accounts were simply disbelieved. Reporters treated police reports as highly credible and often relayed them as factual accounts. Yet video evidence of police brutality shows that the claims of communities of color were more credible than police assertions of benevolence, equality, or colorblindness. Black Americans' counternarrative of highlighting disproportionate police brutality against Black communities isn't what's novel about these videos. Black Americans were already experts on their experiences with police harassment. These videos' novelty lies in having Black people's counternarrative—a narrative that better comports with empirical reality—corroborated by hard-to-refute recordings.[7]

Critical race theory takes seriously the stories of people of color, analyzing discrimination from the perspectives of racism's targets, not its perpetrators. Centering the targets' experiences of racism is a radical departure from standard practice. Racism, as an ideology of human worth, necessarily discounts the opinions, ideas, and emotions of its targets. Part of this discounting includes dismissing claims about racism's impact. Drawing on narratives, parables, and personal stories, critical race theorists disrupt taken-for-granted accounts of the causes and consequences of racial inequality and center the experiences of those—in Derrick Bell's famous phrase—"at the bottom of the well."[8] This doesn't mean that the accounts of people of color are invariably correct, or that their opinions are homogeneous.

But, on average, people of color have a better understanding of the experiences and consequences of structural racism.

Analogously, the #MeToo movement showed how the routine dismissal of women's accounts of sexual violence is a key factor allowing patriarchal violence to continue. Valorizing the narratives of powerful men over the reports of their victims, the media and law enforcement refused to hold men such as Bill Cosby and Harvey Weinstein accountable. Similarly, denying the experiences of discrimination and unequal treatment of people of color is a central cog in the machinery of structural racism. Critical race theorists center the narratives of people of color as both an affirmation that their perspectives matter (and are often correct) and an empathetic bridge across racial divides.

CHALLENGING AMERICA'S DOMINANT STORIES

The stories America tells about itself are weighted on a racial "hierarchy of credibility," as the sociologist Howard Becker described our propensity to believe those with greater power or higher status.[9] Messages are not interpreted independently of the messenger, and those at the top of social hierarchies, such as bosses in the workplace, professors during lectures, or generals in the military, are typically given deference. In the workplace or classroom, refusing to fall in line and accept the view of reality dictated from the top results in getting fired or failed. Anyone who has worked for a boss knows that those at the top of a hierarchy aren't always correct and don't always know what's best. Bosses, generals, and professors routinely make errors. It isn't the bosses' ideas, the generals' charisma, or the professors' wit but their relative power that compels obedience.

Hierarchies of credibility distort reality because they encourage believing the powerful and discounting the accounts of the relatively powerless, the marginalized, or social outcasts. Racism is a hierarchical system whose victims are disempowered, dehumanized, and disbelieved. Discounting the voices of the racially marginalized was (and remains) a feature of the American legal system. Prior to the passing of the Fourteenth Amendment, the enslaved couldn't testify against their enslavers, and in some free states, Black people couldn't testify against whites.[10] Jim Crow laws often ensured that Black people's testimonies were either inadmissible or easily ignored (if, indeed, Black people were brave enough to testify against whites because doing so could get them murdered). Notorious all-white juries acquitted unquestionably guilty white lynching parties—such as Emmett Till's killers—when they were brought to trial at all.[11] Such acquittals aren't historical relics of less enlightened times. Narratives of Black criminality and white fear were central to the not-guilty verdict that let George Zimmerman walk after he killed Trayvon Martin and to former officer Darren Wilson facing no charges after shooting Mike Brown.

The sense that Black people can't be objective on race matters leads to their legal exclusion from juries. Although the Supreme Court ruled it unconstitutional to bar a juror based on their race in *Batson v. Kentucky,* some prosecutors have developed an array of creative colorblind excuses for removing nonwhites.[12] According to Gilad Edelman, the farce of race neutrality in juror removals for traits like "too old, too young; living alone, living with a girlfriend" led one Illinois judge to quip, "New prosecutors are given a manual, probably entitled, 'Handy Race-Neutral Explanations' or '20 Time-Tested Race-Neutral Explanations.'"[13] Excluding Black jurors isn't a hypothetical harm, as juries drawn from all-white pools are 16 percent more likely to convict Black defendants. Including just one Black person in a jury pool eliminates this disparity.[14] Racial hierarchies of credibility also shape courtroom interactions. As sociologist Nicole Gonzalez Van Cleve shows in her critical race analysis of Chicago's Cook County courthouses, judges and prosecutors routinely subject Black and Latino defendants to dehumanizing "racial degradation rituals" that undermine their testimonies, for instance by mocking Black vernacular English or Black names.[15]

Scholarship, which is used to set policy, also discounts the voices of people of color.[16] In "Imperial Scholar," Richard Delgado showed how the perspectives of people of color were even minimized in the area of civil rights law.[17] Surveying top law reviews for cutting-edge work on protecting minority rights, Delgado discovered that a small group of white scholars dominated the literature. Delgado argued that excluding members of marginalized groups, through intent or accident, from having some say on laws designed to protect their interests had implications for the laws' effectiveness. Dominant group members may lack important information about group norms, they may be ineffective champions of minority group interests, or they may even come to be seen as group spokespersons, making advocacy from group members more difficult in the future. None of these factors imply any malice on the part of the civil rights scholars. Delgado simply recognized that exclusion shapes collective understandings of group priorities and civil rights as much as inclusion.

Stories can capture how racism saturates social life in consequential ways that legal remedies can't or don't touch. Concepts such as discrimination or even structural racism often miss how racist ideas are woven into America's cultural fabric and are not easily amenable to legal recourse. In "The Id, the Ego, and Equal Protection," Charles R. Lawrence III discusses the impact of being the only Black child in an integrated classroom when *The Story of Little Black Sambo* was read to the class.[18] Sambo is a notoriously racist caricature of a Black child. As the book was being read, Lawrence was seized by a deep discomfort, claiming,

"I wish I could disappear." Recall that convincing evidence in the *Brown* decision was partially based upon the Dolls Test, which showed the harmful psychological impact of segregation on Black children. In a culture where racism infects even children's stories, integration may provide Black students with access to resources while simultaneously exposing them to new psychological harms. Lawrence's story also shows the contextual nature of racial progress, as thirty years later while he was taking his daughter to school, a "pink-faced" boy wanted to share his favorite book, handing Lawrence a copy of *The Story of Little Black Sambo*. Today's anti–critical race theory crusaders would condemn racially marginalized kids to thirty (or more) years of erasure and distorted narratives. They have attempted, for instance, to ban books such as *The Story of Ruby Bridges* (which tells the true story of a six-year-old Black girl integrating an all-white school after *Brown*) and *Martin Luther King, Jr. and the March on Washington*.[19]

Qualitative sociologists who rely on interview and observational data have long appreciated the power of personal accounts explaining the impact of the law and social policy on individuals. Statistics on mass incarceration help to explain the scope and scale of the problem. But the detached language of social science often obscures the impact of incarceration on individuals and their families. Narratives from those who have experienced incarceration can show imprisonment's impact, humanizing people who have passed through a dehumanizing system. In his book *Halfway Home: Race, Punishment, and the Afterlife of Mass Incarceration,* Dr. Reuben Miller deftly shows how personal stories can illuminate the multiple cascading costs of mass incarceration.[20] By sharing the stories of formerly imprisoned people, including his own brother, Dr. Miller illustrates the long-lasting afterlife of incarceration on nearly every aspect of post-prison life. Miller describes a web of arbitrary rules that govern the formerly incarcerated, shaping daily routines, and how a slight violation can lead to re-imprisonment. This web is Kafkaesque, as people are released from prison with no place to live, but homelessness is a parole violation. Miller's respondents recount how the stresses of navigating these arbitrary burdens make staying out of prison difficult and fray family bonds. When Dr. Miller's brother was released from prison, the many advantages Dr. Miller had accrued as a professor at one of the nation's most prestigious universities couldn't offset the constraints of the criminal justice system. The apartment Dr. Miller secured for his brother fell through, because the roommate had large dogs, which the parole officer considered potentially dangerous weapons.

Critics of critical race theory's method of drawing on stories, parables, and counternarratives argue that the technique falsely homogenizes people of color, flattening intra-racial variations. But shared social experiences don't mean people will invariably draw similar conclusions from those experiences. Both Supreme Court justice Clarence Thomas and some proponents of critical race theory draw on Malcolm X's Black nationalism—which focused on self-reliance and keeping resources within the Black community—to inform their analysis. Justice Thomas uses the most reactionary parts of Malcolm's legacy to call for cutting the safety net and for armed self-defense.[21] Critical race theorists such as Gary Peller draw on Malcolm's nationalism to argue for the need to rethink the liberal assimilationist paradigm that erases elements of Black identity by expecting conformity to white norms in the name of racial progress.[22] Similarly, Bell's early work criticized a split within the civil rights movement, claiming Black middle-class lawyers weren't always responsive to the needs of working-class Black Americans who wanted better educational conditions for their children—not necessarily integration.

Critical race theory's use of narrative to center the stories of people of color is a corrective to dominant white-washed stories that justify and harm. Contra the notion that critical race theory's use of the stories of people of color is homogenizing, incorporating these stories challenges erasure and forces a recognition of heterogeneous perspectives.

CHAPTER 8

RACIALIZED ORGANIZATIONS

One might have expected a huge controversy over the dramatic
social transformation necessary to eradicate the regime of American apartheid. By and large, however, the very same whites who
administered explicit policies of segregation and racial domination kept their jobs as decision makers in employment
offices of companies, admissions offices of schools,
lending offices of banks, and so on.

KIMBERLÉ CRENSHAW ET AL.[1]

The contemporary American landscape is populated with
organizations that arose under, and profited from, a legal
regime of racial apartheid. Ivy League schools such as Harvard, Yale, and Brown were not only founded with proceeds from the slave trade[2] but also funded the development
of insidious eugenic thinking that remains the backbone of
white supremacist thought.[3] Large portions of the American system of land-grant universities, which helped to
democratize higher education for white Americans, are
built upon proceeds from stolen land. The Morrill Act took
10.7 million acres of land from 250 Indigenous groups
and sold it to fund endowments for fifty-two land-grant

universities, including elite schools like the Massachu-setts Institute of Technology.[4] Wall Street's early trading included human property. Mortgages on the enslaved helped fund westward expansion, and enslaved labor produced the cotton that fueled the industrial revolution.[5] Manage-ment techniques developed on plantations were also use-ful for controlling factory workers.[6] The racial hierarchies developed and built into organizational processes under slavery and Jim Crow are reflected in contemporary board-rooms and broom closets.

Race is a fundamental social relationship that influences the likelihood that an organization will form and how long an organization will survive. American workplaces, schools, and churches remain highly segregated. Discrimination shapes who is likely to get a job; where a person is likely to end up in a workplace hierarchy; how employees, practitio-ners, or students are likely to interact; and many other mun-dane features of organizations that appear, at first glance, as race neutral.[7] Many universities, which tout their com-mitment to diversity and inclusion, have quietly dropped race-conscious admissions.[8] People of color remain clus-tered near the bottom of many integrated organizations; Black and Latino people are less likely to be hired (in both entry- and higher-level jobs) and they move up the hierar-chy more slowly than equally qualified white people.

Racial inequalities in organizations span ideological di-vides, as the most liberal organizations in American society are as racially stratified as conservative ones, if not more so.[9] Universities are routinely criticized for being bastions of liberal thought, yet racial underrepresentation among both students and faculty has remained high even after 1960s desegregation. Silicon Valley tech companies such as Apple and Google consistently fall short of their diversity goals, and their organizational hierarchies are deeply stratified by race.[10] Even the Southern Poverty Law Center—an organization founded to confront white supremacy—has been criticized for an internal culture that marginalizes the very people of color the organization was founded to support.[11] The problem of racism in organizations isn't somewhere "out there" that managers, administrators, and leaders can ignore. "Race is not merely in organizations, but of them," as collective organizations shape racial meanings, provide a context for discrimination (or acceptance), and shape social mobility.[12]

ORGANIZATIONS ARE RACIAL STRUCTURES

Racialized organizations theory, which focuses on the centrality of organizations in producing racial inequality, is my relatively recent addition to critical race theory. Racialized organizations theory is concerned with how racial processes shape organizations in ways both obvious and obscure. Collective organizations such as workplaces, schools, churches, and nonprofits are where society makes, consolidates, accumulates, and distributes resources. And because organizations are designed to outlive their creators, many of the processes (and problems) that organizations create are long-lasting. Race-neutral thinking about organizations, at best, makes racial inequalities hard to see by hiding and legitimating racial inequality. At worst, it ends up blaming people of color for their own victimization.

Racialized organizations theory argues that organizations shape agency between racial groups. Organizations (intentionally and unintentionally) unequally distribute resources based upon racial group membership. By so doing, organizations shape the ability to plan and accomplish future goals. Agency seems like an abstract concept, but organizations are key to social mobility and social incorporation, as full (or partial) membership in collective organizations shapes an individual's chances of actualizing imagined futures.

Modern notions of race as a category of social division emerged under slavery and colonialism to justify constraining the agency of nonwhite groups. Racial categories developed on the plantation consigned Black people to servitude, delineating who worked and who reaped the benefits of labor. Jim Crow was designed to limit Black people's ability to navigate every organization they interacted with. Separate water fountains weren't (just) about refreshment, and separate train cars weren't just about travel. Segregated amenities were a constant reminder that Black ambition would be checked, and likely thwarted, by white power. Educational segregation—from elementary school through higher education—limited (and still limits) the career choices of non-whites, the ability to exercise basic rights, the ability to control the fruits of one's labor, or even to choose a fulfilling occupation. Hiring discrimination—which is widespread—means it takes Black people more time to find work, and pay differentials mean it takes more time to buy groceries, pay off loans, and buy a home.

Unequal incorporation into nominally integrated organizations can also produce profound racial inequalities. Agency-limiting acts can come from gatekeepers, as in the famous story in *The Autobiography of Malcolm X* when he was told by a teacher that Black boys couldn't be lawyers.[13] Or agency can be limited through more obscure means, such as locating jobs in areas without public transportation, making work difficult to access for highly segregated workers.[14] If hired, people of color are more likely to be assigned highly variable schedules, making it difficult to plan time with family or accomplish other goals.[15] Notions of merit, and who is considered "leadership material," are allegedly neutral, but whiteness often acts as an unspoken organizational credential, easing one's bureaucratic passage. The credential of whiteness is apparent when, for instance, Asian Americans with elite educations and impeccable workplace histories hit the "bamboo ceiling," curtailing further advancement. Intentionally or by accident, organizational processes can limit one's ability to act upon the world.[16]

A recent study on structural racism in healthcare shows how racial inequality can be built into organizational processes and have a staggeringly large impact. Hospitals increasingly rely on predictive algorithms to help diagnose illnesses and target treatments. These algorithms are proprietary, and often a single company's software becomes the industry standard, adopted across the entire healthcare field. This widespread adoption can affect millions of patients. Boosters and companies argue that, as mathematical functions, algorithms are race-neutral decision-making tools, and promote them to reduce costs, human error, and racial biases that impact diagnosis and treatment.

But algorithms aren't race neutral.[17] Adopting algorithms to intervene in racial inequality doesn't eliminate bias; it automates bias.[18] Algorithms are trained on data with a history of baked-in structural racism that can be incredibly harmful for sick Black people. Researchers recently discovered an algorithm that was systematically underreporting Black folks' level of illness. Because of historical inequality between Blacks and whites in healthcare provisioning, American healthcare organizations have, on average, spent more money to keep white people healthy. By training an algorithm on healthcare spending data, the designers imported historical racial inequalities into a con-

temporary healthcare provisioning tool.[19] The implications
of this problem were grave, potentially leading to Black patients receiving less care at equal or worse levels of sick-
ness. The scale of institutionalized bias was massive, as the
researchers who discovered this problem claimed this type
of predictive algorithm was applied to more than 200 million patients a year. This is an example of how the decisions
of a single organization, adopted and implemented across
many other organizations, can have an impact on society-
wide racial inequality. Racialized organizations can magnify the reach of structural racism by adopting, spreading,
and legitimating biased procedures.

Just as some states found legal ways to subvert voting
rights in the face of changing laws, organizations can undermine policies that are aimed at intervening in racial inequality, such as diversity programs. Diversity replaced
affirmative action as a rationale for promoting integrated
organizations following Supreme Court justice Lewis Powell's opinion in *Regents of the University of California v. Bakke*.
Allan Bakke was a white engineer whose legal team argued
that affirmative action unconstitutionally denied him ad-
mission to the University of California at Davis medical
school. The *Bakke* decision banned the use of racial quotas
in admissions. Powell's opinion also established that the
state had a compelling interest in promoting a diverse student body. This compelling interest meant schools could
therefore continue to consider race as one factor in a holis-

tic admissions process. Importantly, Powell's opinion in *Bakke* rejected the traditional rationales of slavery, Jim Crow, or ongoing racial discrimination as reasons to diversify. In line with Bell's interest convergence thesis (see chapter 5), Powell focused on the shared educational benefits of diversity for both whites and people of color. Diversity is a nebulous concept that equates highly politicized identities (race) with relatively benign ones (region of origin). Powell's opinion domesticated diversity, helping to make it palatable by detaching the concept from a commitment to righting historical injustice.

Following *Bakke,* many organizations claim to support diversity in principle. But diversity policies have done little to change the overall distribution of racial power within organizations. Despite widespread perceptions that Black professionals are sought after, they remain underrepresented in positions of power. White men remain at the top of most workplace hierarchies, in the most high-status and well-paid jobs, and progress on Black-white occupational segregation "essentially stopped after 1980."[20] High-status firms select employees from elite schools whose pool of nonwhite students is limited. Many of these firms see diversity primarily as a public relations exercise, not as a moral or business imperative.[21] Organizations have even reshaped legal responses to civil rights law, capturing and subverting the very laws designed to stop discrimination. For some organizations, having a diversity program *is the whole program,* as courts have blunted the impact of antidiscrimination law by ruling that the presence of antidiscrimination programming—regardless of that programming's effectiveness at stopping discrimination—is a good-faith effort and can protect companies from legal liability.[22]

Like critical race theory more broadly, racialized organizations theory draws attention to how the daily, mundane functions of organizations reproduce racial inequality. This approach may seem less provocative than focusing on areas that are usually thought of as the primary vehicles of structural racism, such as the criminal justice system. But racialized organizations' role in distributing resources unequally along racial lines is as important, if not more important, in producing our society's profound racial inequalities. The insidious regularity of working in segregated jobs, attending segregated schools, or worshipping in segregated churches reflects a normalized acceptance of inequality. Organizationally produced racial inequalities channel agency and choices, and even shape life expectancy, as workplace risks are shifted onto nonwhites. Racial inequality isn't an exceptional state: racial inequality is normal and produced through often mundane, invisible, and taken-for-granted organizational practices. Racialized organizations socialize participants into seeing structural racism as an unquestioned background feature of American life.

CHAPTER 9

INTERSECTIONALITY

And my own use of the term "intersectionality" was just a metaphor. I'm amazed at how it gets over- and underused; sometimes
I can't even recognize it in the literature anymore. I was simply
looking at the way all these systems of oppression overlap. But
more importantly, how in the process of that structural convergence rhetorical politics and identity polities—based on the idea
that systems of subordination do not overlap—would abandon issues and causes and people who actually were affected by overlapping systems of subordination. I've always been interested in
both the structural convergence and the political marginality.

KIMBERLÉ CRENSHAW[1]

The history of progressive social movements is simultaneously a history of eclipsed visions of freedom. Suffragists
who pushed for women's right to vote were heroic by almost any measure. Confronting the patriarchal powers of
their day, they sought to expand democracy by institution-
alizing women's greater participation in their government.
Yet some suffragist unwillingness to see Black men enfran-
chised partially obscured their view of liberation. Susan B.
Anthony opposed the franchise for Black men despite Fred-
erick Douglass's entreaty to her to support the Fifteenth
Amendment while continuing to fight for the vote for

women. She said, "I would cut off my right arm before I would ever work or demand the ballot for the negro."[2]

An incomplete vision of democratic incorporation also marred the heroism of the civil rights movement. Months before Rosa Parks's history-making refusal, Claudette Colvin, a Black teenager, refused to relinquish her seat when a bus driver ordered her to make room for a white passenger. But in contrast to Rosa Parks's middle-class respectability, Colvin was working-class and pregnant with a white man's baby. Fearing white supremacist opponents would use Colvin's status to discredit the movement, local activists passed on this opportunity to challenge Montgomery's segregation order.[3] Organizers of the March on Washington also succumbed to exclusionary politics when Bayard Rustin, who helped tutor Dr. King in Gandhian nonviolent civil disobedience, wasn't allowed to direct the march for fear that his queerness and prior association with communism would be weaponized against the movement.[4] In each of these cases, a single axis of oppression was seen as the primary terrain of struggle. Those whose identities fell outside these norms were further marginalized by liberation movements.

Intersectionality, as both a structural theory of oppression and a broader political program, attempts to move past the shortcomings of visions of freedom that rely on others' exclusion or erasure. Recognizing that all of us live at the intersection of racial, gender, and class-based structural hierarchies, intersectionality begins with the understanding that liberation can't be partial. By promoting solutions that don't get caught on the shoals of particularity or allow one aspect of identity to take priority over another, intersectional theorists are committed to freedom in the broadest sense. Acknowledging that progressive social movements' visions of democracy are partial doesn't take away from their accomplishments. Yet intersectional theorists know that partial notions of inclusion deny our full humanity and threaten everyone's rights. In Dr. King's oft-quoted phrase, "Injustice anywhere is a threat to justice everywhere."[5]

INTERSECTIONALITY AND LEGAL INVISIBILITY

Kimberlé Crenshaw developed the concept of intersectionality in a sequence of groundbreaking articles in the late 1980s and early 1990s: "Demarginalizing the Intersection of Race and Sex: A Black Feminist Critique of Antidiscrimination Doctrine, Feminist Theory and Antiracist Politics" and "Mapping the Margins: Intersectionality, Identity Politics, and Violence Against Women of Color." Crenshaw's early discussions of intersectionality show why one-size-fits-all approaches to solving social problems often fail or end up further marginalizing people whose identities challenge dominant ideas about who is worthy of legal and social recognition.

In "Demarginalizing," Crenshaw analyzes the case of five Black women who were suing General Motors for relief from the impact of ongoing discrimination. Rather than focusing on unfair treatment because of either their race or their gender, of necessity, they chose to sue "not on behalf of Blacks or women, but specifically on behalf of Black women."[6] Like many American companies, before 1964 General Motors simply didn't hire Black women. GM did, however, hire both white women and Black men. When implementing seniority-based layoffs during a recession, the company let go all Black women hired after 1970. Seniority-based layoffs are colorblind policies that don't discriminate based on race or gender. Yet decades of gendered racism in hiring and promotion meant that General Motors policy created durable structures of intersectional exclusion. The plaintiffs were suing for relief from the combined impact of these structures.

In deciding this case, the court was stuck thinking about discrimination along a single identity-based axis. General Motors' policy excluded the category of Black women—who existed at the intersection of multiple marginalized categories—which led to their being laid off. Yet, the court denied the women's claim, holding that sex discrimination hadn't occurred because GM hired white women prior to 1964. And the court dismissed the plaintiffs' race discrimination claim, suggesting that they join a different race discrimination claim against GM that was proceeding separately. Worried about creating a special category of protection for Black women that would potentially open the door to subsequent, as-yet-unimagined legal redress, the court ignored that those intersecting categories already existed, compounding these women's marginalization.

In "Mapping the Margins: Intersectionality, Identity Politics, and Violence Against Women of Color," Crenshaw extends her analysis of intersectionality to women of color more broadly, showing how the routine violence of racism and patriarchy combines to impact women's lives.[7] Crenshaw highlights how aspects of immigration policy—specifically the marriage fraud provisions of the Immigration Act of 1990—were potentially yoking vulnerable immigrant women to abusive partners.

Marriage fraud provisions required two years of marriage to a U.S. citizen before an immigrant could apply for permanent resident status. By linking naturalization to marriage, immigrant women of color were sometimes forced to choose between staying with an abusive partner and deportation. Crenshaw also shows how the normative whiteness of the women's shelter movement could occasionally lead shelters to "fail at their own goals" by not taking intersectionality into account. Domestic violence shelters were an important innovation of the feminist movement. By creating a safe space for women and their children fleeing violence, shelters provided a critical route to escape mortal danger. Crenshaw lauds the goals and accomplishments of the movement but cites a shelter's English-only policy as a blind spot that undermined feminist goals. Crenshaw shows how exclusionary language policies, which required English proficiency, forced a woman fleeing abuse to live in danger on the street because she spoke Spanish. Like the women's suffrage and civil rights movements, whose visions of freedom were truncated by narrow thinking, the shelter movement ignored the combined impacts of multiple marginalization, fell short of their goals, and exposed women of color to the very harms their movement hoped to minimize. Liberatory policies need to be expansive, flexible, and intersectional to avoid reinforcing oppressive structures.

THE BLACK FEMINIST ROOTS
OF INTERSECTIONALITY

Although Kimberlé Crenshaw is credited with coining the term "intersectionality," the notion that women of color face multiple barriers to full participation in American society has a long intellectual lineage among Black feminist scholar-activists. Black feminist scholar-activists were in solidarity with other women whose potential was limited by sexist social expectations and with men of color whose experiences of racism shaped their life chances. As progenitors of intersectionality, these scholar-activists went beyond single-issue analyses, showing where their experiences converged with, and differed from, other types of structural discrimination. Sojourner Truth's famous "Ain't I a Woman" speech at the 1851 Women's Rights Convention illustrated how race complicated gendered ideas about the supposed gallantry showered upon women. Sojourner Truth noted that her experiences as a Black woman, whose labor was stolen and whose children were sold into slavery, couldn't easily be compared to those of white women, who were "helped into carriages, and lifted over ditches, and to have the best place everywhere."[8] Similarly, in 1892, Anna Julia Cooper noted that Black women faced "both a woman question and a race problem," whose solutions required thinking about American democratic inclusion in the broadest possible terms. Cooper also recognized that Black women's diminished economic position was the result of combined class and gender oppression.[9] Ida B. Wells showed that the terror of lynching was often rooted in economic competition but drew on gendered and racialized scripts for justification. White men assaulted Black women in the Jim Crow South with impunity, while lies about Black men's hypersexuality were used to excuse ritualized murder.[10] All of these Black feminist thinkers recognized that single-issue analyses of race or gender often efface the concerns of people living at the intersection of multiple marginalized categories.

The Black feminists of the Combahee River Collective (named for a Civil War raid led by Harriet Tubman, which freed hundreds of enslaved people) built upon prior analyses and their personal experiences as Black feminist lesbians to outline possibilities for political solidarity through shared experiences of social exclusion. Among the collective's members were women who went on to make important contributions to academia and politics, including the sisters Barbara and Beverly Smith and the writer Audre Lorde. Drawing on their history of organizing in the Black Power, New Left, and mainstream civil rights movements, Combahee critiqued prior movements for ignoring Black women's political concerns. The civil rights movement often focused on the concerns of middle-class Black Americans who wanted, among other things, equal access to white consumer spaces. Dr. Martin Luther King Jr. recognized this critique when he reflected on the gains of the civil rights movement by saying, "What does it profit a man to be able to eat at an integrated lunch counter if he doesn't earn enough money to buy a hamburger and a cup of coffee?"[11] The white feminist movement wanted, among other things, access to work in spaces that had historically excluded white women—Black feminists pointed out that Black women had always worked, oftentimes in the homes of white women (which provided white women space for leisure).

The women of Combahee understood that the single-issue foci of prior movements were insufficient. In 1974 the collective wrote a classic revolutionary statement now recognized as a precursor to intersectionality, arguing that systems of oppression are interlocking and that Black women have always been involved in struggles for equality, despite mainstream white organizations paying little attention to them. They wrote:

> We are actively committed to struggling against racial, sexual, heterosexual, and class oppression, and see as our particular task the development of integrated analysis and practice based upon the fact that the major systems of oppression are interlocking. The synthesis of these oppressions creates the conditions of our lives.[12]

As scholar-activists, they were not trying to simply describe the problem but to develop a maximally liberatory politics drawing on Black women's experiences. In a kind of trickle-up theorizing, Combahee argued that focusing on the problems of those simultaneously marginalized by multiple systems of structural oppression would help develop expansive solutions to social problems. Policies designed to empower those at the bottom would lead to greater freedoms for everyone. Combahee was committed to finding solidarity across difference by acknowledging shared humanity. In contrast to a politics that uses identity to close off opportunity and understanding, Combahee used identity as a starting place to communicate across— rather than solidify—social divides.

Public debates have drifted well beyond Crenshaw's initial formulation of intersectionality as a framework for understanding how overlapping structures of oppression shape opportunities. Indeed, Crenshaw claims she finds some public renditions of intersectionality unrecognizable because they deviate so sharply from the original conceptualization. Writing about the language of totalitarianism, Masha Gessen notes that concepts describing the operation of power are threatening to autocratic regimes, so they attempt to obliterate thought by mangling the meaning of words.[13] Conservative critics of intersectionality (and critical race theory more generally) have adopted this autocratic strategy by misrepresenting intersectionality's meaning, attempting to strip its liberatory potential by stigmatizing and delegitimating the concept. Conservatives who intentionally confuse intersectionality's meaning re-create the political marginality Crenshaw mentioned in this chapter's epigraph, erasing Black women from the theory and recentering white men. For instance, Ben Shapiro claims "the original articulation of the idea by Crenshaw is accurate and not a problem." Yet he fears that intersectionality creates a "hierarchy of victimhood" devaluing white men's opinions.[14] Shapiro's worries implicitly acknowledge key contentions of intersectionality—that racial identities shape our opinions and that white men's opinions are currently well represented, considering they remain firmly at the top of American media hierarchies.

Intersectionality arose from Black feminist concerns about multiple forms of political exclusion. The theory acknowledges that our experiences are partial, but aims to create inclusive policies and practices free from the kinds of domination and exclusion that have shaped prior movements. Conservatives' anxiety over intersectionality reveals a real fear that their own position is based not solely on meritocracy or skill but rather on structural advantages that eased (and partially determined) their ascent.

CHAPTER 10

IDENTITY POLITICS

When there is massive unemployment in the
black community, it's called a social problem. But when
there is massive unemployment in the white community, it's
called a depression. With the black man, it's "welfare," with the
whites it's "subsidies." This country has socialism for the rich,
rugged individualism for the poor.

DR. MARTIN LUTHER KING JR.[1]

In my classes on racial inequality, I assign works for students to read in parallel: a classic academic article introducing a concept and a popularization of that concept. Typically, the academic article is Peggy McIntosh's "White Privilege: Unpacking the Invisible Knapsack," which shows how unquestioned white norms shape basic aspects of daily life—such as white overrepresentation in movies and magazines—in ways that are often invisible to people at the top of America's racial hierarchy.[2] McIntosh makes a strong case that whiteness reduces the frictions of daily life (being able to cash checks without being challenged, not having one's educational credentials questioned) and creates slight, invisible advantages. Students recognize that the article promotes introspection and empathy and they don't feel implicated or accused. I pair this with one of the many published articles that misrepresent white privilege as a concept developed to demean whites and their accomplishments, such as Tal Fortgang's "Why I'll Never Apologize for My White Male Privilege."[3] Fortgang tells the compelling history of his family's escape from Nazi Germany, but dodges McIntosh's argument while pretending to refute it. Nothing in McIntosh's article claims whites never experience adversity; rather, privilege is probabilistic and contextual. The concept of white privilege arose from a different intellectual tradition than critical race theory, but its concerns with normative ideas about race are resonant, as are mainstream misrepresentations of the ideas.

My students, often white and working-class, get the point of this exercise immediately. Intentionally or by accident, when ideas move from academia to the public, meaning and nuance are often lost or erased. And popularizers with a political agenda don't necessarily represent academic arguments faithfully, or in line with the empirical evidence. In the case of white privilege, this lack of fidelity to the source material may come from the popularizers' opposition to the idea that Black and white people are treated differently in public. Many white Americans are deeply opposed to admitting the game is rigged. Research from 2011 indicates that a slim majority of whites believed (contrary to all evidence) that anti-white discrimination is a bigger problem than anti-Black discrimination.[4] The researchers attribute this finding to perceptions of decreasing animosity toward nonwhites, coupled with whites' zero-sum thinking about race, which together lead whites to the conclusion that anti-white animus has increased. More charitably than rejecting evidence, unfamiliarity with the norms of academic debate can lead to misrepresentation. The concept of identity politics, in moving from activist circles, through academia, and eventually into the mainstream, is a striking example of how ideas become distorted as they travel across contexts.

THE USES AND ABUSES OF IDENTITY POLITICS

The Black feminists of the Combahee River Collective (discussed in the last chapter) developed the concept of identity politics to describe a political program that would address their specific needs as Black women. Savvy political visionaries, the Combahee River Collective recognized that successful political organizing is coalitional, and developed a program to connect across social differences. They argued that "the most profound and potentially most radical politics come directly out of our own identity," and planned to use that radical vision to build universal political solutions promoting maximum freedom.[5]

Combahee's conception of identity politics as a tool for

making universal policy is almost entirely at odds with how the term has come to be deployed. Mainstream discussions of identity politics drop the aspirations for universal freedom and replace them with a narrow and exclusionary meanness. These critics paint the concerns of people of color, women, and the LGBTQ community as distractions from economic fundamentals that should propel both collective identity and political action. Right-wing critiques of identity politics rely on projection, claiming that a focus on marginalized identities will lead to a "reverse racism" against whites.[6] Left-wing critics paint the concerns of people of color, women, and the LGBTQ community as distractions from economic fundamentals that should propel both collective identity and political action. These critiques are premised on misrepresentation, as Combahee's intent to acknowledge Black women's historically extreme levels of economic deprivation inspired their attention to identity in the first place. But Combahee recognized that a narrow focus on class often erased the ways that economic oppression worked in concert with gender and race. Recently, Barbara Smith addressed these misrepresentations, announcing her support for Bernie Sanders during the 2020 presidential campaign. Smith claimed that Sanders's economic policy was in line with Combahee's vision and provided the best chance to "eradicate the unique injustices that marginalized groups in America endure."[7]

For critical race theorists, the problem with identity

politics isn't social groups arguing for their interests. Fighting for one's perceived interest is, after all, central to politics (although critical race theorists draw a distinction between the right to exclude and expansive notions of full inclusion). And the successes of civil rights and women's campaigns show the potential utility of organizing around shared identity-based experiences and exclusions.

The problem with identity politics, Kimberlé Crenshaw says, is not "that it fails to transcend difference, but rather the opposite—that it frequently conflates or ignores intra-group differences," as privileged group members tend to dominate political agenda-setting, marginalizing the positions of their fellow group members.[8] Olúfẹ́mi O. Táíwò calls the tendency of the powerful to set political boundaries for the rest of us "elite capture" and notes that the process "is a general feature of politics, anywhere and everywhere," not specific to marginalized groups.[9] Derrick Bell pointed to this problem when he recognized that civil rights lawyers suing for school integration were often at political odds with the parents they represented.[10] Many Black parents wanted greater resources for their children's education and were either agnostic on segregation or (realistically) recognized that some white parents would never support full desegregation. Yet Black middle-class lawyers set an agenda for desegregation that comported with their class interests. More recently, Michelle Alexander attributed the civil rights community's slow recognition of the problem of mass incarceration to elite capture. Black civil rights lawyers were relatively unlikely to be imprisoned, and they recognized that the widespread association between Blackness and criminality would make organizing difficult.[11] The point here is not to rehash arguments over which political strategy made the most sense; it is that group members with the most power and resources tend to set political agendas, making their *particular* preferences seem universal.

WHITE IDENTITY POLITICS

When it comes to political agenda-setting, white identity politics are the most successful identity politics in American history. The success of white identity politics rests upon an entrenched white normativity that refuses to see whiteness as a political identity and white interests as politics. In the mainstream media white Americans are positioned as a default, universal, neutral category. Against this white baseline—considered just politics—the needs of people of color are considered "special interests." This tendency is more pronounced among Republicans, whose devotion to white identity politics is often overt, vulgar, and increasingly includes elements of explicit white supremacist ideology.[12] The Democrats' constituency is a multiracial coalition. Nonetheless, pundits and Democratic consultants regularly warn the party that catering to the needs of minority constituents is political suicide likely to alienate white Democrats and swing voters. And although they have much less power to shape political discussions, even socialists downplay racial inequality, focusing on supposedly more fundamental issues of economic inequality. As with the identity politics of marginalized groups, white identity politics often bolster the relative position of the most privileged (think here of regressive tax policies). Nonetheless, the material benefits accruing from inclusion in white identity politics have been significant enough that Charles Mills claims "race is the identity around which whites have usually closed ranks" when given the opportunity to form cross-racial solidarity.[13]

The normativity of white identity politics shows up through representation in American public life generally. From the start of the Trump campaign, national papers such as *The New York Times* ran a series of interviews with salt-of-the-earth white Americans in diners. Readers were encouraged to empathize with these so-called "real Americans," whose support for an openly racist candidate was justified by a narrative of "economic anxiety" that explained away their acceptance of bigotry.

Even the term "working class" is often conflated with ideas about white and male workers, despite people of color being overrepresented in working-class jobs. According to the historian David Roediger, the industrial white working class arose and defined their collective identity in partial opposition to the idea of bonded labor (this opposition even shapes our language, as the word "boss"—from the Dutch—was adopted as a way for whites to avoid calling their superiors "master," even though the words are synonyms).[14] The identity politics of the white working class made wage labor itself a white prerogative, and positioned white men above people of color in workplace hierarchies. Contemporary organizations that replicate these hierarchies show the remarkable staying power of white prerogative in having access to good jobs.

Academics, too, spend quite a bit of time explaining white identity politics. The sociologist Arlie Hochschild's *Strangers in Their Own Land: Anger and Mourning on the American Right*—a National Book Award–nominated book— argued that we should empathize with white Americans who feel left behind by changing social norms. Hochschild examined the so-called "deep stories" that conservative white Americans tell themselves.[15] These Americans see their successes in terms of hard work, effort, and deservingness— rather than the structural advantages that allowed them to accrue wealth and resources. When describing the outcomes of those historically denied access to government largesse because of their race, Hochschild's respondents victim-blame, claiming that the relative lack of success of people of color isn't the result of discrimination and structural racism but a supposedly inferior work ethic. Similarly, economists' research on whites' declining life expectancy in the face of changing economic conditions—which re-

searchers dubbed "deaths of despair"—encouraged sympa-
thy for a group of Americans whose whiteness is assumed
to provide some insulation against the worst economic
chills.[16] As Ta-Nehisi Coates writes, white people's down-
ward trajectories inspired a flurry of commentary "devoted
to the sympathetic plight of working-class whites when
their life expectancy approaches levels that, for blacks, society simply accepts as normal."[17]

The narrative of white decline is compelling. Economic
dislocations have indeed left behind many white Americans. Concerns regarding America's catastrophic levels of
economic inequality are legitimate, and empathy with everyone impacted by brutal economic policy decisions is
proper. But this empathy is rarely extended to people of
color, whose lack of employment prospects and histories of
structural exclusion are both longer-lasting and more se-
vere. But, as Coates and others have pointed out, commentators primarily ignored (or blamed) the communities of
color that were ground zero for policies whose fallout has
now descended on whites. Often, these communities are
the state's testing ground for economic pain and political
repression later visited on white communities. Commentators who (rightly) focus on the pain of white workers—
while minimizing the equally (or more) legitimate claims
of communities of color—ignore that many whites supported the destruction of the safety net they now need.

Even the mainstream definitions of racism are shaped

by white identity politics. Focusing on narrow attitudes and beliefs absolves participants' complicity in wider systems that produce racial inequality. Narrow definitions of racism also cloud the analysis of overt acts that fall short of using racial slurs. For instance, in covering Trump's many racist statements, the same media companies that helped create the narrative of economic anxiety driving white support for him avoided using the descriptively accurate terminology to characterize the former president's language. Worried that they would be accused of bias, these papers held endless debates over the proper use of the word "racism," in relation to Trump's rhetoric and policy. This refusal to accurately describe reality is a kind of white identity politics masquerading as journalistic objectivity. Pointing out the ridiculous circumlocutions of the mainstream press's racism-avoidant language, historian Lawrence Glickman cites a *New York Times* headline claiming, "Trump and G.O.P. Candidates Escalate Race and Fear as Election Ploys." Glickman wryly asks, "How exactly does one 'escalate race'?"[18] Throughout Trump's campaign and presidency, euphemisms such as "racially charged," "racially tinged," or "nationalist" stood in for the clear, descriptive terms "racist" or "white nationalist." These colorblind editorial choices were likely motivated by a desire to avoid appearing biased or potentially upsetting white readers and losing market share. These choices ignored the concerns of communities of color targeted by rising white nationalism, and allowed white identity politics to set their editorial agenda, by using a definition of racism that conveniently absolves most racist actions.

It is a strange conception of politics that sees Black Americans—at the bottom of most social indicators—as asking for special favors based on their identity when white Americans control nearly every industry. Identity politics have always been central to American ideals about deservingness and inclusion. And denying that whites engage in identity politics is itself a form of identity politics. Liberals who traffic in the myth of economic interests untainted by racial antipathy reinforce tropes about marginalized communities' basic rights to make claims on their government. White identity politics shape whose interests are considered "special" and whose goals aren't considered politics at all.

It can sound trite to say that all politics are identity politics. But if we recognize that marginalized groups advocating for their interests is identity politics, symmetry and logical consistency require a similar recognition when it comes to whites' priorities. White identity politics see white interests and identities as the norm and attempt to distribute social and material resources accordingly. White identity politics often operate under a false cover of universality. But white Americans have been able to institutionalize their self-interest by controlling national narratives in the arts, politics, and media. White identity politics are more than the explicit ideology of neo-Nazis or the Klan. Because these politics are connected to how many people see and understand the world and the distributive processes of states and organizations, many people who explicitly reject white supremacist ideology nonetheless receive material and psychological benefits from white identity politics.

Contemporary attacks on critical race theory are themselves a kind of identity politics attempting to restore a nationalist narrative of white innocence. As the political scientist Don Moynihan points out, there is something unseemly about white men with no expertise or training in race scholarship making national reputations by attempting to tarnish the intellectual production of scholars of color.[19] The activists who started this moral panic recognize that critical race counternarratives empower racially marginalized groups by providing a clear explanation of America's racial structure. And these activists know that clear explanation can undermine the policies and practices that they have unfairly benefited from.

I would be remiss to avoid discussing how my politics were shaped by my identity. I've experienced considerable social mobility over the course of my lifetime. And I try to be a consistent structuralist by acknowledging how access to white spaces facilitated that mobility. Like Cheryl Harris's grandmother, whose story is recounted in the chapter on whiteness as property (chapter 6), my own access to white spaces has exposed me to the hidden racism of daily life, and the blatant double standards around merit and access to resources that are foundational to American society. As a teenager first reading Malcolm X's autobiography, I understood Malcolm's description of the deep bitterness those of us who can pass sometimes feel.[20] Malcolm X claimed that access to whites' racial backstage left us with few illusions about the depths and routine nature of interpersonal racism. Witnessing the hypocrisy up close makes it clear that hard work and perseverance are rarely enough, in the aggregate, to overcome the sheer waste and brutality of the political system of structural racism.

Identity politics shape *all sides* of America's abiding color lines. The illusion that dominant groups' politics are somehow free from identity obscures (and helps to perpetuate) their hold on power. Critical race theory shatters the illusion that identity politics are limited to racially subordinated groups, threatening the unequal distribution of resources and power that this illusion helped to produce and justify.

AGAINST THE PROPAGANDA OF HISTORY

If you can control a man's thinking you do not have to worry
about his actions. When you determine what a man shall think
you do not have to concern yourself about what he will do. If you
make a man feel that he is inferior, you do not have to compel
him to accept an inferior status, for he will seek it himself. If you
make a man think that he is justly an outcast, you do not have to
order him to the back door. He will go without being told; and if
there is no back door, his very nature will demand one.

CARTER G. WOODSON[1]

I wrote the first draft of this book in a three-month sprint,
attempting to outrun the anti–critical race theory laws
spreading across the United States. These laws were built
upon the rickety frame of former president Trump's 2020
executive order that claimed critical race theory was "un-
American" and banned even tepid diversity trainings un-
connected to the theory. Disinformation (and outright lies)
about critical race theory were flooding the public sphere,
and the media seemed ill-equipped to separate fact from
propaganda. I knew the best primers on critical race theory—
like Kimberlé Crenshaw and colleagues' classic volume of
foundational texts, *Critical Race Theory: The Key Writings*

That Formed the Movement[2] and Richard Delgado and Jean Stefancic's *Critical Race Theory: An Introduction*[3]—were aimed at academics. It was disconcerting to see unscrupulous grifters weaponize important research and minimize the seriousness of racial inequality. I thought the public needed a concise, accessible explanation that presented key concepts clearly—and fast. Perhaps paradoxically for a writer, while working on the first draft I hoped for a small audience. Scant attention would mean the moral panic around critical race theory was subsiding, a goal more important than book sales.

Critical race theory matters because it helps explain the intractable nature of America's particular brand of structural racism. Critical race theory unmasks race-neutral language that provides a plausibly deniable cover for racist intent and outcomes. Critical race theory explains how the biological fiction of race has justified some of the world's worst tragedies. Critical race theory shows how organizations—imbued with meanings about the proper place of racialized bodies—distribute resources and shape agency. Critical race theory refuses the narcotic mythologies of inevitable racial progress and unimpeachable white innocence. Critical race theory shows how living at the intersection of multiple marginalized categories can compound inequality. Critical race theory shows how the property interest in whiteness has contributed to unfathomable wealth gaps. And critical race theory challenges those at the top of America's racial hierarchies by illuminating the causes and consequences of racism that mainstream discussions intentionally obscure.

Unfortunately, as this book goes to press, the autocratic lurch in American politics hasn't dissipated. President Joe Biden repealed the executive order banning diversity training shortly after taking office. But conservatives, looking for future electoral victories through stoked racial animus, doubled down on their caricature of critical race theory. A century after W.E.B. Du Bois diagnosed "the deliberately educated ignorance of white schools," some white parents and politicians are attempting to ensure children's ignorance.[4] What started as a set of laws targeting critical race theory has metastasized into a series of broader nationalist attacks on who belongs in a multiracial democracy. State legislators in Texas are targeting LGBTQ literature, attempting to get hundreds of books removed from syllabi and library shelves. And a school board in Tennessee even removed Art Spiegelman's *Maus*, the classic Pulitzer Prize–winning graphic novel on the Holocaust's generational impact. These laws have been forwarded under the pretext that these works make white kids uncomfortable, and discomfort is to be avoided. But America's history is disturbing, and a healthy society would be disturbed. Banning discussions of structural racism is an unforgivably cruel *type of structural racism* designed to deny marginalized people both the affirmation that comes from learning their stories matter and the conceptual tools that help them understand and alter their position.

Critical race theory also reminds us that white supremacist law, policy, and practice didn't bind only people of color. The political system of structural racism also polices whites' behavior, sometimes compelling whites who were reluctant to participate in biased systems, too. Laws barring interracial marriage helped keep white people out of relationships that might have undermined Jim Crow's rigid color line. Restrictive covenants were designed to coerce white homeowners' economic decisions by making it illegal to sell their property to Black families, and redlining compelled white banks to lend to white people within specified racially segregated communities.[5] Acting outside of, or against, the system of structural racism carried potential costs. As this book makes clear, the political system of structural racism does not hurt everyone equally. The data on racial inequality is unequivocal that white Americans, on average, have disproportionately benefited. But by compelling participation in the dehumanization of nonwhites, white supremacy warped the morality of both its passive and its active beneficiaries.[6] Legislative attacks on critical race theory are contemporary updates of laws designed to compel participation in structural racism. Teachers, educators, and college professors are professionally committed to facts, inquiry, and verification. These commitments are an inherent threat to folks who want to spread what W.E.B.

Du Bois called the "propaganda of history."[7] If there is any solace to be taken from the moral panic over critical race theory, it is that the attacks are coming from a position of weakness. The conservative think tanks and propagandists feel threatened, and they are worried that demographic and ideological change will loosen their grip on power.

Critical race theory is an intellectual bulwark against the propaganda of history. Multiracial democracy is a recent and fragile innovation in American history. Those who think this fact has no place in our schools would—intentionally or not—hasten a return to unquestioned white dominance. We should never forget that it took National Guard soldiers to get Black and white kids seated together in American schools, that abstract notions of a colorblind Constitution weren't a shield against slavery's horrors or the savagery of lynching, that Jim Crow was a legal regime codifying racial subordination, and that civil rights wrested from white supremacy's stingy fingers could be snatched back.

ACKNOWLEDGMENTS

This book would not have come together so quickly without a ton of support. My agent, Sarah Burnes at the Gernert Company, plucked me out of her timeline by following up on my semi-joking tweet about pitching a short, punchy book on critical race theory. Thank you for taking a risk, reaching out, and changing my future. Jamia Wilson not only provided crucial editorial direction and brilliant feedback but also talked me through blocks and put up with my somewhat erratic email responses. The entire team at Penguin Random House was incredible to work with, but I want to give special thanks to Darryl Oliver for keeping me together and on task.

Ideas are always developed in community with other thinkers. Critical race theorists and some sociologists have supported me throughout my career. I want to thank Richard Delgado and Jean Stefancic for taking the time to talk with Louise Seamster and me, and for introducing us to Derrick Bell when we were undergraduates. I didn't realize the gift you were giving us at the time, but I now try to emulate the model that you showed us of being generous with time. I was lucky enough to have two graduate advisors who continue to have my back. Dr. Eduardo Bonilla-Silva has been a hilarious and committed advisor who taught me that there is more than one way to do sociology and told me to shape the career that I wanted, not what the discipline expected from me. Dr. Linda Burton has guided me through every professional and many personal decisions, never wavering in her commitment to making the world kinder.

The Ford Foundation saved me twice (so far), by providing funding during grad school and again when I needed to reevaluate my career trajectory. And I want to thank the Department of Sociology and Criminology and program in African American studies at the University of Iowa for giving me the space and resources I needed to complete this work. Maddie Libao, Carson Byrd, Jeff Guhin, Ted Thornhill, and Max Jordan Nguemeni Tiako provided early comments on sections of the book and moral support. Aldon Morris, Rashawn Ray, and Nicole Gonzalez Van Cleve provided me with forums to discuss some of the ideas that made it into the book before I knew it would become a book. Raúl Pérez, Antar A. Tichavakunda, Alan Aja, and Danté Stewart took time to speak with me or answer questions at pivotal moments, and I'm thankful. Steven Thrasher and Rob Tolliver listened to me vent and reminded me that many things matter more than work.

My family makes everything possible. Thanks, Mom and Dad, for teaching me not to back down from racists but rather to go for their neck. My life is daily enriched by Louise Seamster's brilliance, and I am lucky that she shares it with me. And Malcolm, if you ever read this book, I hope it is during a time when books like this are less necessary.

NOTES

PREFACE

1. Kimberlé Crenshaw, "Twenty Years of Critical Race Theory: Looking Back to Move Forward," *Connecticut Law Review* 43 (2010): 1253–1352, 1352.

2. Although *Loving v. Virginia* overturned antimiscegenation laws nationwide in 1967, many states kept these laws on the books for decades after they were declared unconstitutional. Alabama was the last state to remove them, in the year 2000.

3. Lori D. Patton, Berenice Sánchez, Jacqueline Mac, and D-L Stewart, "An Inconvenient Truth About 'Progress': An Analysis of the Promises and Perils of Research on Campus Diversity Initiatives," *Review of Higher Education* 42, no. 5 (2019): 173–98.

4. Raúl Pérez, *The Souls of White Jokes: How Racist Humor Fuels White Supremacy* (Redwood City, CA: Stanford University Press, 2022).

5. Leslie Houts Picca and Joe R. Feagin, *Two-Faced Racism: Whites in the Backstage and Frontstage* (New York: Routledge, 2007).

6. Victor Ray and Danielle Purifoy, "The Colorblind Organization," in *Race, Organizations, and the Organizing Process,* edited by Melissa E. Wooten, vol. 60 in *Research in the Sociology of Organizations* (Emerald, 2019), 131–50.

7. Michelle Alexander, *The New Jim Crow: Mass Incarceration in the Age of Colorblindness* (New York: New Press, 2012).

8. Carol Anderson, *One Person, No Vote: How Voter Suppression Is Destroying Our Democracy* (New York: Bloomsbury Publishing USA, 2018).

9. Jasmine Banks, "The Radical Capitalist Behind the Critical Race Theory Furor," *The Nation,* August 13, 2021.

10. Adam Serwer, "Birtherism of a Nation," *The Atlantic,* May 13, 2020.

11. Timothy Snyder, *On Tyranny: Twenty Lessons from the Twentieth Century* (New York: Tim Duggan Books, 2017).

12. Jason Stanley, *How Fascism Works: The Politics of Us and Them* (New York: Random House, 2018).

13. Rebecca C. Hetey and Jennifer L. Eberhardt, "The Numbers Don't Speak for Themselves: Racial Disparities and the Persistence of Inequality in the Criminal Justice System," *Current Directions in Psychological Science* 27, no. 3 (2018): 183–87.

INTRODUCTION

1. Anatole France, *The Red Lily,* vol. 1 (New York: J. Lane, 1910), 95.

2. James Baldwin, "As Much Truth as One Can Bear," *New York Times,* January 14, 1962.

3. Derrick A. Bell Jr., "*Brown v. Board of Education* and the Interest-Convergence Dilemma," *Harvard Law Review* 93, no. 3 (1980): 518–33.

4. Nikole Hannah-Jones, "Segregation Now," *The Atlantic,* May 15, 2014, 58–69.

5. Lincoln Quillian, Devah Pager, Ole Hexel, and Arnfinn H. Midtbøen, "Meta-Analysis of Field Experiments Shows No Change in Racial Discrimination in Hiring over Time," *Proceedings of the National Academy of Sciences* 114, no. 41 (October 10, 2017): 10870–75; John-Paul Ferguson and Rembrand Koning, "Firm Turnover and the Return of Racial Establishment Segregation," *American Sociological Review* 83, no. 3 (June 2018): 445–74.

6. Kevin Stainback and Donald Tomaskovic-Devey, *Documenting Desegregation: Racial and Gender Segregation in Private-Sector Employment Since the Civil Rights Act* (New York: Russell Sage Foundation, 2012).

7. Amaka Okechukwu, *To Fulfill These Rights: Political Struggle over Affirmative Action and Open Admissions* (New York: Columbia University Press, 2019).

8. Kimberlé Crenshaw, "Twenty Years of Critical Race Theory: Looking Back to Move Forward," *Connecticut Law Review* 43 (2010): 1253–1352.

9. Ibid., 1265.

10. Jelani Cobb, "The Limits of Liberalism," *New Yorker,* September 20, 2021, 20–26, 22.

11. Ian Haney López, *White by Law: The Legal Construction of Race,* 10th anniv. ed. (New York: NYU Press, 2006).

12. Jacey Fortin, "Critical Race Theory: A Brief History," *New York Times,* November 8, 2021.

13. Douglas Massey and Nancy A. Denton, *American Apartheid: Segregation and the Making of the Underclass* (Cambridge, MA: Harvard University Press, 1993); Thomas J. Sugrue, *The Origins of the Urban Crisis* (Princeton, NJ: Princeton University Press, 2014); Robert D. Bullard, *Dumping in Dixie: Race, Class, and Environmental Quality* (New York: Routledge, 2018).

14. Hakeem Jefferson and Victor Ray, "White Backlash Is a Type of Racial Reckoning, Too," FiveThirtyEight, January 6, 2022.

15. Jennifer Chudy and Hakeem Jefferson, "Opinion: Support for Black Lives Matter Surged Last Year. Did It Last?" *New York Times,* May 22, 2021.

16. Jennifer C. Mueller, "Producing Colorblindness: Everyday Mechanisms of White Ignorance," *Social Problems* 64, no. 2 (2017): 219–238.

17. Charles Mills, "White Ignorance," in *Race and Epistemologies of Ignorance,* ed. Nancy Tuana and Shannon Sullivan (Albany: State University of New York Press, 2007): 13–38, 13.

18. Sarah Schwartz, "Map: Where Critical Race Theory Is Under Attack," *Education Week,* June 11, 2021.

19. David J. Silverman, "Perspective: The Battle over Critical Race Theory Is as American as Pumpkin Pie," *Washington Post,* November 24, 2021.

20. Sarah Jones, "How to Manufacture a Moral Panic," *Intelligencer,* July 11, 2021.

21. Laura Meckler and Josh Dawsey, "Republicans, Spurred by an Unlikely Figure, See Political Promise in Critical Race Theory," *Washington Post,* June 19, 2021.

22. Linda Gordon, *The Second Coming of the KKK: The Ku Klux Klan of the 1920s and the American Political Tradition* (New York: Liveright, 2018).

23. Josh Harkinson, "Meet the White Nationalist Trying to Ride the Trump Train to Lasting Power," *Mother Jones* (blog), October 26, 2016.

24. David Waldstreicher, *Slavery's Constitution: From Revolution to Ratification* (New York: Farrar, Straus and Giroux, 2010).

25. Ezra Klein, interview with Nikole Hannah-Jones and Ta-Nehisi Coates, *The Ezra Klein Show* (podcast), July 30, 2021.

26. Ibram X. Kendi, *Stamped from the Beginning: The Definitive History of Racist Ideas in America* (New York: Nation Books, 2016).

27. Mae M. Ngai, "The Architecture of Race in American Immigration Law: A Reexamination of the Immigration Act of 1924," *Journal of American History* 86, no. 1 (1999): 67–92, 70.

28. Lee D. Baker, *From Savage to Negro* (Oakland: University of California Press, 1998).

29. Ngai, "The Architecture of Race in American Immigration Law."

30. James Whitman, *Hitler's American Model: The United States and the Making of Nazi Race Law* (Princeton, NJ: Princeton University Press, 2017).

31. Jia Lynn Yang, *One Mighty and Irresistible Tide: The Epic Struggle Over American Immigration, 1924–1965* (New York: W. W. Norton, 2020).

32. Adam Serwer, "Jeff Sessions's Unqualified Praise for a 1924 Immigration Law," *The Atlantic*, January 10, 2017.

33. Steven Levitsky and Daniel Ziblatt, *How Democracies Die* (New York: Crown, 2018).

34. Eric Foner, *The Second Founding: How the Civil War and Reconstruction Remade the Constitution* (New York: W. W. Norton, 2019).

35. Kendi, *Stamped from the Beginning*.

36. Isabel Wilkerson, *The Warmth of Other Suns: The Epic Story of America's Great Migration* (New York: Random House, 2010).

37. Robin D. G. Kelley, *Freedom Dreams: The Black Radical Imagination* (Boston: Beacon Press, 2002).

38. Wells was bombarded with death threats and driven from her Memphis, Tennessee, home for her anti-lynching activism. Walter White passed as white to collect evidence on lynching from the Klan. See Paula J. Giddings, *Ida: A Sword Among Lions: Ida B. Wells and the Campaign Against Lynching* (New York: HarperCollins, 2009); Walter White, *A Man Called White: The Autobiography of Walter White* (Athens: University of Georgia Press, 1995).

39. David A. Graham, "Breitbart.com's Massive Barack Obama–Derrick Bell Video Fail," *The Atlantic*, March 8, 2012.

40. Heather McGhee, *The Sum of Us: What Racism Costs Everyone and How We Can Prosper Together* (New York: One World, 2021).

41. Adam Serwer, "The Fight over the 1619 Project Is Not About the Facts," *The Atlantic,* December 23, 2019.

42. Crenshaw, "Twenty Years of Critical Race Theory," 1253.

43. Devon W. Carbado and Daria Roithmayr, "Critical Race Theory Meets Social Science," *Annual Review of Law and Social Science* 10, no. 1 (November 3, 2014): 149–67.

44. Michelle Christian, Louise Seamster, and Victor Ray, "New Directions in Critical Race Theory and Sociology: Racism, White Supremacy, and Resistance," *American Behavioral Scientist* 63, no. 13 (2019): 1731–40.

45. Victor Erik Ray, Antonia Randolph, Megan Underhill, and David Luke, "Critical Race Theory, Afro-Pessimism, and Racial Progress Narratives," *Sociology of Race and Ethnicity* 3, no. 2 (2017): 147–58.

Chapter 1

1. W.E.B. Du Bois, *Dusk of Dawn: An Essay Toward an Autobiography of a Race Concept* (Piscataway, NJ: Transaction, 2011), 153.

2. William I. Thomas and Dorothy S. Thomas, *The Child in America* (New York: Alfred A. Knopf, 1928), 72.

3. Michael Omi and Howard Winant, *Racial Formation in the United States* (New York: Routledge, 2014).

4. Alan Goodman, "Two Questions About Race," in "Is Race 'Real'? A Web Forum Organized by the Social Science Research Council," 2006.

5. Jean Beaman, "France's Ahmeds and Muslim Others: The Entanglement of Racism and Islamophobia," *French Cultural Studies* 32, no. 3 (2021): 269–79; Jean Beaman and Amy Petts, "Towards a Global Theory of Colorblindness: Comparing Colorblind Racial Ideology in France and the United States," *Sociology Compass* 14, no. 4 (April 2020).

6. Adrienne LaFrance, "The Prophecies of Q," *The Atlantic,* May 14, 2020.

7. Kevin Roose, "What Is QAnon, the Viral Pro-Trump Conspiracy Theory?" *New York Times,* September 3, 2021.

8. Quoted in Dorothy Roberts, *Fatal Invention: How Science, Politics, and Big Business Re-create Race in the Twenty-first Century* (New York: Free Press, 2011), 50.

9. Melissa Nobles, *Shades of Citizenship: Race and the Census in Modern Politics* (Redwood City, CA: Stanford University Press, 2000); G. Cristina Mora, "Cross-Field Effects and Ethnic Classification: The Institutionalization of Hispanic Panethnicity, 1965 to 1990," *American Sociological Review* 79, no. 2 (April 2014): 183–210.

10. Joseph L. Graves Jr., *The Race Myth* (New York: Dutton, 2004).

11. Alan H. Goodman and Joseph L. Graves Jr., *Racism, Not Race: Answers to Frequently Asked Questions* (New York: Columbia University Press, 2021).

12. Wendy D. Roth and Biorn Ivemark, "Genetic Options: The Impact of Genetic Ancestry Testing on Consumers' Racial and Ethnic Identities," *American Journal of Sociology* 124, no. 1 (July 2018): 150–84.

13. Peggy Pascoe, "Miscegenation Law, Court Cases, and Ideologies of 'Race' in Twentieth-Century America," *Journal of American History* 83, no. 1 (June 1, 1996): 44–69, 54.

14. W.E.B. Du Bois, "The Souls of White Folk," in *Darkwater: Voices from Within the Veil* (New York: Dover, 2012).

15. Dorothy Roberts, "Race," in *The 1619 Project: A New Origin Story,* created by Nikole Hannah-Jones and *The New York Times Magazine* (New York: One World, 2021).

16. F. James Davis, *Who Is Black? One Nation's Definition* (University Park: Penn State University Press, 2010).

17. James Whitman, *Hitler's American Model: The United States and the Making of Nazi Race Law* (Princeton, NJ: Princeton University Press, 2017), 77.

18. Davis, *Who Is Black?*

19. James R. Browning, "Anti-Miscegenation Laws in the United States," *Duke Bar Journal* 1 (1951): 27–29.

20. Michael Omi, "Racial Identity and the State: The Dilemmas of Classification," *Minnesota Journal of Law & Inequality* 15, no. 1 (1997): 7–23.

21. D. R. Roediger, *Working Toward Whiteness: How America's Immigrants Became White: The Strange Journey from Ellis Island to the Suburbs* (New York: Basic Books, 2005); M. F. Jacobson, *Whiteness of a Different Color* (Cambridge, MA: Harvard University Press, 1999).

22. Keisha N. Blain, *Until I Am Free: Fannie Lou Hamer's Enduring Message to America* (Boston: Beacon Press, 2021), 35.

23. Dorothy Roberts, *Killing the Black Body: Race, Reproduction, and the Meaning of Liberty* (New York: Vintage Books, 1998), 91.

24. Adam Cohen, *Imbeciles: The Supreme Court, American Eugenics, and the Sterilization of Carrie Buck* (New York: Penguin Press, 2016), 23.

CHAPTER 2

1. Quoted in George Lipsitz, *The Possessive Investment in Whiteness: How White People Profit from Identity Politics* (Philadelphia: Temple University Press, 2018), 199.

2. Kerner Commission, *Report of the National Advisory Commission on Civil Disorders* (Washington, DC: Government Printing Office, 1968).

3. Kimberlé Crenshaw, Neil Gotanda, Gary Peller, and Kendall Thomas, eds., *Critical Race Theory: The Key Writings That Formed the Movement* (New York: New Press, 1996).

4. Ellen Berrey, Robert L. Nelson, and Laura Beth Nielsen, *Rights on Trial: How Workplace Discrimination Law Perpetuates Inequality* (Chicago: University of Chicago Press, 2017).

5. Elizabeth Korver-Glenn, "Compounding Inequalities: How Racial Stereotypes and Discrimination Accumulate Across the Stages of Housing Exchange," *American Sociological Review* 83, no. 4 (August 2018): 627–56.

6. Victor Ray and Alan Aja, "Racism Isn't About Ignorance. Some Highly Educated People Have Upheld Systemic Inequality," *Washington Post,* June 18, 2020.

7. Charles W. Mills, *The Racial Contract* (Ithaca, NY: Cornell University Press, 1997).

8. Victor Ray, "A Theory of Racialized Organizations," *American Sociological Review* 84, no. 1 (February 2019): 26–53.

9. Kwame Ture and Charles V. Hamilton, *Black Power: The Politics of Liberation* (New York: Vintage Books, 1992), 4.

10. Jo C. Phelan and Bruce G. Link, "Is Racism a Fundamental Cause of Inequalities in Health?" *Annual Review of Sociology* 41, no. 1 (August 14, 2015): 311–30.

11. Darrick Hamilton and William A. Darity Jr., "The Political Economy of Education, Financial Literacy, and the Racial Wealth Gap," *Federal Reserve Bank of St. Louis Review* 99, no. 1 (2017): 59–76; Alan A. Aja and Michelle Holder, *Afro-Latinos in the U.S. Economy* (Lanham, MD: Lexington Books, 2021).

12. Melvin L. Oliver and Thomas M. Shapiro, *Black Wealth/White Wealth: A New Perspective on Racial Inequality* (New York: Routledge, 1997).

13. Eduardo Bonilla-Silva, Carla Goar, and David G. Embrick, "When Whites Flock Together: The Social Psychology of White Habitus," *Critical Sociology* 32, no. 2–3 (March 2006): 229–53.

14. Amanda E. Lewis, "'What Group?' Studying Whites and Whiteness in the Era of 'Color-Blindness,'" *Sociological Theory* 22, no. 4 (December 2004): 623–46.

15. Ruth Wilson Gilmore, *Golden Gulag: Prisons, Surplus, Crisis, and Opposition in Globalizing California* (Oakland: University of California Press, 2007), 28.

16. Naa Oyo A. Kwate, "The Race Against Time: Lived Time, Time Loss, and Black Health Opportunity," *Du Bois Review: Social Science Research on Race* 14, no. 2 (2017): 497–514.

17. Shannon M. Pruitt, Donna L. Hoyert, Kayla N. Anderson, Joyce Martin, Lisa Waddell, Charles Duke, Margaret A. Honein, and Jennita Reefhuis, "Racial and Ethnic Disparities in Fetal Deaths— United States, 2015–2017," *Morbidity and Mortality Weekly Report* 69, no. 37 (September 18, 2020): 1277–82.

18. "Infant Mortality and African Americans," U.S. Department of Health and Human Services, Office of Minority Health, 2021.

19. Robert L. Goldenberg and Jennifer F. Culhane, "Low Birth Weight in the United States," *American Journal of Clinical Nutrition* 85, no. 2 (February 1, 2007): 584S–90S.

20. David R. Williams and Michelle Sternthal, "Understanding Racial/ Ethnic Disparities in Health: Sociological Contributions," *Journal of Health and Social Behavior* 51, Suppl. (2010): S15–27.

21. Gloria Ladson-Billings and William F. Tate IV, "Toward a Critical Race Theory of Education," *Teachers College Record* 97 (1995): 47–68.

22. Jonathan Kozol, *The Shame of the Nation: The Restoration of Apartheid Schooling in America* (New York: Three Rivers Press, 2005).

23. Gary Orfield and Danielle Jarvie, "Black Segregation Matters: School Resegregation and Black Educational Opportunity," *Civil Rights Project–Proyecto Derechos Civiles,* 2020.

24. Linda Darling-Hammond, *Education and the Path to One Nation, Indivisible* (Palo Alto, CA: Learning Policy Institute, 2018).

25. Walter S. Gilliam, *Prekindergarteners Left Behind: Expulsion Rates in State Prekindergarten Systems* (New York: Foundation for Child Development, 2005).

26. Monique W. Morris, *Pushout: The Criminalization of Black Girls in Schools* (New York: New Press, 2016), 77.

27. Jason A. Okonofua and Jennifer L. Eberhardt, "Two Strikes: Race and the Disciplining of Young Students," *Psychological Science* 26, no. 5 (May 2015): 617–24.

28. Amanda E. Lewis, John B. Diamond, and Tyrone A. Forman, "Conundrums of Integration: Desegregation in the Context of Racialized Hierarchy," *Sociology of Race and Ethnicity* 1, no. 1 (January 2015): 22–36.

29. James W. Ainsworth-Darnell and Douglas B. Downey, "Assessing the Oppositional Culture Explanation for Racial/Ethnic Differences in School Performance," *American Sociological Review* 63, no. 4 (August 1998): 536–53; John B. Diamond and James P. Huguley, "Testing the Oppositional Culture Explanation in Desegregated Schools: The Impact of Racial Differences in Academic Orientations on School Performance," *Social Forces* 93, no. 2 (December 1, 2014): 747–77.

30. Renee Stepler, "Hispanic, Black Parents See College Degree as Key for Children's Success," Pew Research Center, February 24, 2016.

31. Valerie Wilson and William M. Rodgers III, "Black-White Wage Gaps Expand with Rising Wage Inequality," Economic Policy Institute, September 19, 2016; Amanda E. Lewis and John B. Diamond, *Despite the Best Intentions: How Racial Inequality Thrives in Good Schools,* Transgressing Boundaries: Studies in Black Politics and Black Communities (New York: Oxford University Press, 2015).

32. Olugbenga Ajilore, "The Persistent Black-White Unemployment Gap Is Built into the Labor Market," *Center for American Progress* (blog), September 28, 2020.

33. Dara Z. Strolovitch, "Of Mancessions and Hecoveries: Race, Gender, and the Political Construction of Economic Crises and Recoveries," *Perspectives on Politics* 11, no. 1 (March 2013): 167–76.

34. Adam Storer, Daniel Schneider, and Kristen Harknett, "What

Explains Racial/Ethnic Inequality in Job Quality in the Service Sector?" *American Sociological Review* 85, no. 4 (August 2020): 537–72.

35. S. Michael Gaddis, "Discrimination in the Credential Society: An Audit Study of Race and College Selectivity in the Labor Market," *Social Forces* 93, no. 4 (June 2015): 1451–79.

36. Berrey, Nelson, and Nielsen, *Rights on Trial*.

37. Rebecca M. Blank, Marilyn Dabady, and Constance F. Citro, eds., *Measuring Racial Discrimination* (Washington, DC: National Academies Press, 2004).

38. Ian Ayres and Peter Siegelman, "Race and Gender Discrimination in Bargaining for a New Car," *American Economic Review* 85, no. 3 (1995): 304–21.

39. Devah Pager and Hana Shepherd, "The Sociology of Discrimination: Racial Discrimination in Employment, Housing, Credit, and Consumer Markets," *Annual Review of Sociology* 34, no. 1 (2008): 181–209.

40. Devah Pager, Bart Bonikowski, and Bruce Western, "Discrimination in a Low-Wage Labor Market: A Field Experiment," *American Sociological Review* 74, no. 5 (October 2009): 777–99.

41. Devah Pager, "The Mark of a Criminal Record," *American Journal of Sociology* 108, no. 5 (2003): 937–75.

42. Devah Pager and Lincoln Quillian, "Walking the Talk? What Employers Say Versus What They Do," *American Sociological Review* 70, no. 3 (June 2005): 355–80.

43. Marianne Bertrand and Sendhil Mullainathan, "Are Emily and Greg More Employable Than Lakisha and Jamal? A Field Experiment on Labor Market Discrimination," *American Economic Review* 94, no. 4 (2004): 991–1013.

44. Richard V. Reeves and Christopher Pulliam, "No Room at the Top:

The Stark Divide in Black and White Economic Mobility," *Brookings* (blog), February 14, 2019.

45. Victor Ray, Pamela Herd, and Donald Moynihan, "Racialized Burdens: Applying Racialized Organization Theory to the Adminis-trative State," *Journal of Public Administration Research and Theory,* January 29, 2022.

Chapter 3

1. Associated Press, "Haldeman Diary Shows Nixon Was Wary of Blacks and Jews," *New York Times,* May 18, 1994.

2. Rick Perlstein, "Exclusive: Lee Atwater's Infamous 1981 Interview on the Southern Strategy," *The Nation,* November 13, 2012.

3. Quoted in Dan Baum, "Legalize It All: How to Win the War on Drugs," *Harper's Magazine,* April 1, 2016, 22–32, 22.

4. Quoted in Khiara M. Bridges, *Critical Race Theory: A Primer* (St. Paul, MN: Foundation Press, 2018), 6.

5. Patricia J. Williams, "Mourning in America," *The Nation,* July 30, 2007, 10.

6. Dorothy A. Brown, *The Whiteness of Wealth: How the Tax System Impoverishes Black Americans—and How We Can Fix It* (New York: Crown, 2021).

7. James Q. Wilson and George L. Kelling, "Broken Windows," *Atlantic Monthly* 249, no. 3 (1982): 29–38.

8. Victor Ray, "Trump's Call for Dystopian Policing," *Boston Review,* October 17, 2016.

9. Michelle Alexander, *The New Jim Crow: Mass Incarceration in the Age of Colorblindness* (New York: New Press, 2012).

10. Angela Y. Davis, *Are Prisons Obsolete?* (New York: Seven Stories, 2011).

11. Ian Haney López, *Dog Whistle Politics: How Coded Racial Appeals Have*

Reinvented Racism and Wrecked the Middle Class (New York: Oxford University Press, 2013).

12. Sarah Mayorga-Gallo, *Behind the White Picket Fence: Power and Privilege in a Multiethnic Neighborhood* (Chapel Hill: University of North Carolina Press, 2014).

13. Alexander, *The New Jim Crow.*

14. Amanda E. Lewis and John B. Diamond, *Despite the Best Intentions: How Racial Inequality Thrives in Good Schools,* Transgressing Boundaries: Studies in Black Politics and Black Communities (New York: Oxford University Press, 2015); Laurie Cooper Stoll, *Should Schools Be Colorblind?* (Hoboken, NJ: Wiley, 2019).

15. Heather McGhee, *The Sum of Us: What Racism Costs Everyone and How We Can Prosper Together* (New York: One World, 2021).

16. López, *Dog Whistle Politics.*

17. Michael Tesler, "How the Rise of White Identity Politics Explains the Fight over Critical Race Theory," *FiveThirtyEight* (blog), August 10, 2021.

18. Alexander, *The New Jim Crow,* 71.

19. Kasey Henricks, "'I'm Principled Against Slavery, but . . .': Colorblindness and the Three-Fifths Debate," *Social Problems* 65, no. 3 (2018): 285–304.

20. Carol Anderson, *One Person, No Vote: How Voter Suppression Is Destroying Our Democracy* (New York: Bloomsbury Publishing USA, 2018); Victor Ray, Pamela Herd, and Donald Moynihan, "Racialized Burdens: Applying Racialized Organization Theory to the Administrative State," *Journal of Public Administration Research and Theory,* January 29, 2022.

21. Eduardo Bonilla-Silva, *Racism Without Racists: Color-Blind Racism and the Persistence of Racial Inequality in America* (Lanham, MD: Rowman & Littlefield, 2017).

22. Quoted in Lincoln Caplan, "Thurgood Marshall and the Need for Affirmative Action," *New Yorker,* December 9, 2015.

23. Clayborne Carson and Kris Shepard, eds., *A Call to Conscience: The Landmark Speeches of Dr. Martin Luther King, Jr.* (Boston: G. K. Hall, 2001), 71.

24. Quoted in Kimberlé Crenshaw, "Playing Race Cards: Constructing a Proactive Defense of Affirmative Action," *National Black Law Journal* 16 (1998): 196.

CHAPTER 4

1. Quoted in Saladin Ambar, *Malcolm X at Oxford Union: Racial Politics in a Global Era,* Transgressing Boundaries: Studies in Black Politics and Black Communities (New York: Oxford University Press, 2014), 122.

2. Koritha Mitchell, "Keep Claiming Space!" *CLA Journal* 58, no. 3/4 (2015): 229–44, 238.

3. Bryan Armen Graham, "Tom Cotton Calls Slavery 'Necessary Evil' in Attack on New York Times' 1619 Project," *The Guardian,* July 26, 2020.

4. Emma G. Fitzsimmons, "Video Shows Cleveland Officer Shot Boy in 2 Seconds," *New York Times,* April 27, 2014.

5. Rishika Dugyala, "2020 Dems Critical of Police Shooting of Woman in Her Home," *POLITICO,* October 13, 2019.

6. Derrick Bell, "Racial Realism," *Connecticut Law Review* 24, no. 2 (1992): 363–80.

7. Victor Ray and Louise Seamster, "Rethinking Racial Progress: A Response to Wimmer," *Ethnic and Racial Studies* 39, no. 8 (2016): 1361–69.

8. Michelle Alexander, *The New Jim Crow: Mass Incarceration in the Age of Colorblindness* (New York: New Press, 2012), 2.

9. Carol Anderson, *One Person, No Vote: How Voter Suppression Is*

Destroying Our Democracy (New York: Bloomsbury Publishing USA, 2018); Ari Berman, *Give Us the Ballot: The Modern Struggle for Voting Rights in America* (New York: Farrar, Straus and Giroux, 2015).

10. Stephen Steinberg, *Turning Back: The Retreat from Racial Justice in American Thought and Policy* (Boston: Beacon Press, 2001).

11. Adam Liptak, "Supreme Court Invalidates Key Part of Voting Rights Act," *New York Times,* June 25, 2013.

12. *Shelby County v. Holder,* 570 U.S., 133 S. Ct. 2612 (2013) at 2650 (Ginsburg, J., dissenting).

13. Keisha L. Bentley-Edwards, Malik C. Edwards, Cynthia N. Spence, William A. Darity Jr., Darrick Hamilton, and Jasson Perez, "How Does It Feel to Be a Problem? The Missing Kerner Commission Report," *RSF: The Russell Sage Foundation Journal of the Social Sciences* 4, no. 6 (2018): 20–40.

14. Ibid.

15. Jacob S. Rugh and Douglas S. Massey, "Racial Segregation and the American Foreclosure Crisis," *American Sociological Review* 75, no. 5 (October 2010): 629–51.

16. George Lipsitz, *The Possessive Investment in Whiteness: How White People Profit from Identity Politics* (Philadelphia: Temple University Press, 2018), xxv.

17. Theresa Andrasfay and Noreen Goldman, "Reductions in 2020 US Life Expectancy Due to COVID-19 and the Disproportionate Impact on the Black and Latino Populations," *Proceedings of the National Academy of Sciences* 118, no. 5 (2021).

18. Jennifer A. Richeson, "Americans Are Determined to Believe in Black Progress," *The Atlantic,* September 15, 2020; Michael W. Kraus, Ivuoma N. Onyeador, Natalie M. Daumeyer, Julian M. Rucker, and Jennifer A. Richeson, "The Misperception of Racial Economic Inequality," *Perspectives on Psychological Science* 14, no. 6 (2019): 899–921.

19. Derrick Bell, *Faces at the Bottom of the Well: The Permanence of Racism* (New York: Basic Books, 2018), xxi.

20. Martin Luther King Jr., "Letter from Birmingham Jail," *Atlantic Monthly* 212, no. 2 (1963): 78–88.

21. David Sirota, "Polls Showed Many Americans Opposed to Civil Rights Protests in the 1960s. But That Changed," *Jacobin*, June 12, 2020.

22. King, "Letter from Birmingham Jail."

23. Bell, "Racial Realism."

Chapter 5

1. *Regents of the University of California v. Bakke,* 438 U.S. 265 (1978) (Marshall, T., dissenting).

2. Derrick Bell, *Faces at the Bottom of the Well: The Permanence of Racism* (New York: Basic Books, 2018).

3. Derrick A. Bell Jr., "*Brown v. Board of Education* and the Interest-Convergence Dilemma," *Harvard Law Review* 93, no. 3 (1980): 518–33.

4. John P. Jackson Jr., *Social Scientists for Social Justice: Making the Case Against Segregation* (New York: NYU Press, 2001).

5. Quoted in Derrick Bell, *Silent Covenants: Brown v. Board of Education and the Unfulfilled Hopes for Racial Reform* (New York: Oxford University Press, 2004), 17.

6. Christopher Bonastia, *Southern Stalemate: Five Years Without Public Education in Prince Edward County, Virginia* (Chicago: University of Chicago Press, 2012).

7. Bell, "*Brown v. Board of Education* and the Interest-Convergence Dilemma," 524.

8. Derrick Bell, *Silent Covenants: Brown v. Board of Education and the Unfulfilled Hopes for Racial Reform* (New York: Oxford University Press, 2004).

9. Mary L. Dudziak,"Desegregation as a Cold War Imperative," *Stanford Law Review* 41, no. 8 (1988): 61–120; Mary L. Dudziak, *Cold War Civil Rights* (Princeton, NJ: Princeton University Press, 2011).

10. Bell, *"Brown v. Board of Education* and the Interest-Convergence Dilemma," 525.

11. Conor Friedersdorf, "The Sci-Fi Story That Offends Oversensitive White Conservatives," *The Atlantic,* March 8, 2012.

12. Elizabeth Wrigley-Field, "US Racial Inequality May Be as Deadly as COVID-19," *Proceedings of the National Academy of Sciences* 117, no. 36 (2020): 21854–56.

13. Drawing on the work of critical race theorist Charles Mills, Adam Serwer argued in May 2020 that the United States' shift in pandemic policy was linked to preliminary research showing the pandemic was disproportionately killing Black and Brown Americans. "The Coronavirus Was an Emergency Until Trump Found Out Who Was Dying," *The Atlantic,* May 8, 2020.

14. Jonathan Metzl, *Dying of Whiteness: How the Politics of Racial Resentment Is Killing America's Heartland* (New York: Basic Books, 2018), 178.

15. Marta W. Aldrich, "Tennessee Nails Down Rules for Disciplining Teachers, Withholding Money from Schools That Teach Banned Concepts About Racism," *Chalkbeat Tennessee,* November 19, 2021.

16. Steven Levitsky and Daniel Ziblatt, *How Democracies Die* (New York: Crown, 2018).

17. Derrick Bell, "The Power of Narrative," *Legal Studies Forum* 23 (1999): 315.

18. Bell, *"Brown v. Board of Education* and the Interest-Convergence Dilemma."

19. Herbert Blumer, "Race Prejudice as a Sense of Group Position," *Pacific Sociological Review* 1, no. 1 (1958): 3–7.

20. Louise Seamster and Victor Erik Ray, "Against Teleology in the

Study of Race: Toward the Abolition of the Progress Paradigm,"
Sociological Theory 36, no. 4 (2018): 315–42.

21. W.E.B. Du Bois, "The Souls of White Folk," in *Darkwater: Voices from Within the Veil* (New York: Dover, 2012).

22. Martin Gilens, *Why Americans Hate Welfare: Race, Media, and the Politics of Antipoverty Policy* (Chicago: University of Chicago Press, 1999).

CHAPTER 6

1. W.E.B. Du Bois, "The Souls of White Folk," in *Darkwater: Voices from Within the Veil* (New York: Dover, 2012).

2. Cheryl I. Harris, "Whiteness as Property," *Harvard Law Review* 106, no. 8 (June 1993): 1707–91.

3. Derrick Bell, *Silent Covenants: Brown v. Board of Education and the Unfulfilled Hopes for Racial Reform* (New York: Oxford University Press, 2004).

4. Courtney L. McCluney, Kathrina Robotham, Serenity Lee, Richard Smith, and Myles Durkee, "The Costs of Code-Switching," *Harvard Business Review,* November 15, 2019.

5. *Plessy v. Ferguson,* 163 U.S. 537, 551 (1896).

6. Karen E. Fields and Barbara Jeanne Fields, *Racecraft: The Soul of Inequality in American Life* (New York: Verso, 2012).

7. *Dred Scott v. Sandford,* 60 U.S. (19 How.) 393 (1857).

8. Frank Wu, *Yellow: Race in America Beyond Black and White* (New York: Basic Books, 2002).

9. David Levering Lewis and W.E.B. Du Bois, *Black Reconstruction in America: An Essay Toward a History of the Part Which Black Folk Played in the Attempt to Reconstruct Democracy in America, 1860-1880,* The Oxford W.E.B. Du Bois (New York: Oxford University Press, 2014). (Kindle edition)

10. Louise Seamster, "Black Debt, White Debt," *Contexts* 18, no. 1 (February 2019): 30–35.

11. Ira Katznelson, *When Affirmative Action Was White: An Untold History of Racial Inequality in Twentieth-Century America* (New York: W. W. Norton, 2005).

12. William A. Darity Jr. and A. Kirsten Mullen, *From Here to Equality: Reparations for Black Americans in the Twenty-first Century* (Chapel Hill: University of North Carolina Press, 2020), 242.

13. Thomas Shapiro, Tatjana Meschede, and Sam Osoro, "The Roots of the Widening Racial Wealth Gap: Explaining the Black-White Economic Divide," *IASP Research and Policy Brief,* 2013.

14. Louise Seamster and Raphaël Charron-Chénier, "Predatory Inclusion and Education Debt: Rethinking the Racial Wealth Gap," *Social Currents* 4, no. 3 (June 2017): 199–207.

15. Devon W. Carbado and Mitu Gulati, *Acting White? Rethinking Race in "Post-Racial" America* (New York: Oxford University Press, 2013).

16. Ted Thornhill, "Racial Salience and the Consequences of Making White People Uncomfortable: Intra-Racial Discrimination, Racial Screening, and the Maintenance of White Supremacy," *Sociology Compass* 9, no. 8 (August 2015): 694–703.

CHAPTER 7

1. Frantz Fanon, *The Wretched of the Earth* (New York: Grove/Atlantic, 1963), 77.

2. Quoted in Megan O'Grady, "These Literary Memoirs Take a Different Tack," *T Magazine,* September 29, 2021.

3. Michael S. Schmidt and Matt Apuzzo, "South Carolina Officer Is Charged with Murder of Walter Scott," *New York Times,* April 7, 2015.

4. John Eligon, Tim Arango, Shaila Dewan, and Nicholas Bogel-Burroughs, "Derek Chauvin Verdict Brings a Rare Rebuke of Police Misconduct," *New York Times,* April 21, 2021.

5. Raygine DiAquoi, "Symbols in the Strange Fruit Seeds: What 'The

Talk' Black Parents Have with Their Sons Tells Us About Racism,"
Harvard Educational Review 87, no. 4 (2017): 512–37.

6. Jeffrey M. Jones, "In U.S., Black Confidence in Police Recovers from
    2020 Low," Gallup, July 14, 2021.

7. Rory Kramer and Brianna Remster, "Stop, Frisk, and Assault? Racial
    Disparities in Police Use of Force During Investigatory Stops," *Law
    & Society Review* 52, no. 4 (2018): 960–93.

8. Derrick Bell, *Faces at the Bottom of the Well: The Permanence of Racism*
    (New York: Basic Books, 2018).

9. Howard S. Becker, "Whose Side Are We On?" *Social Problems* 14
    (1966): 239–47.

10. Amanda Carlin, "The Courtroom as White Space: Racial Perfor-
    mance as Noncredibility," *UCLA Law Review* 63 (2016): 449.

11. Philip Dray, *At the Hands of Persons Unknown: The Lynching of Black
    America* (New York: Random House, 2002).

12. Equal Justice Initiative, *Race and the Jury: Illegal Discrimination in Jury
    Selection* (Montgomery, AL: Equal Justice Initiative, 2021).

13. Gilad Edelman, "Why Is It So Easy for Prosecutors to Strike Black
    Jurors?" *New Yorker,* June 5, 2015.

14. Shamena Anwar, Patrick Bayer, and Randi Hjalmarsson, "The
    Impact of Jury Race in Criminal Trials," *Quarterly Journal of
    Economics* 127, no. 2 (May 1, 2012): 1017–55.

15. Nicole Gonzalez Van Cleve, *Crook County: Racism and Injustice in
    America's Largest Criminal Court* (Redwood City, CA: Stanford
    University Press, 2016).

16. Victor Ray, "The Racial Politics of Citation," *Inside Higher Ed,* April
    27, 2018.

17. Richard Delgado, "Imperial Scholar: Reflections on a Review of
    Civil Rights Literature," *University of Pennsylvania Law Review* 132,
    no. 3 (1984): 561.

18. Charles R. Lawrence III, "The Id, the Ego, and Equal Protection:

Reckoning with Unconscious Racism," *Stanford Law Review* 39, no. 2 (1987): 317–88.

19. Kevin L. Clark, "Right-Wing 'Moms for Liberty' Group Wants 'Anti-American' MLK Jr. Book Banned from Schools," *Essence* (blog), December 3, 2021.

20. Reuben Jonathan Miller, *Halfway Home: Race, Punishment, and the Afterlife of Mass Incarceration* (New York: Little, Brown, 2021).

21. Corey Robin, *The Enigma of Clarence Thomas* (New York: Henry Holt, 2019).

22. Gary Peller, "Race Consciousness," *Duke Law Journal* 1990, no. 4 (September 1990): 758.

CHAPTER 8

1. Kimberlé Crenshaw, Neil Gotanda, Gary Peller, and Kendall Thomas, eds., *Critical Race Theory: The Key Writings That Formed the Movement* (New York: New Press, 1996), xvi.

2. Craig Steven Wilder, *Ebony and Ivy: Race, Slavery, and the Troubled History of America's Universities* (New York: Bloomsbury Publishing USA, 2013).

3. Lee Baker, *From Savage to Negro* (Oakland: University of California Press, 1988).

4. Robert Lee and Tristan Ahtone, "Land-Grab Universities," *High Country News*, March 30, 2020.

5. Matthew Desmond, "American Capitalism Is Brutal. You Can Trace That to the Plantation," *New York Times Magazine*, August 14, 2019.

6. Caitlin Rosenthal, *Accounting for Slavery: Masters and Management* (Cambridge, MA: Harvard University Press, 2018).

7. Victor Ray, "Why So Many Organizations Stay White," *Harvard Business Review*, November 19, 2019.

8. Daniel Hirschman and Ellen Berrey, "The Partial Deinstitutionaliza-

tion of Affirmative Action in U.S. Higher Education, 1988 to 2014," *Sociological Science* 4 (2017): 449–68.

9. Pamela Newkirk, *Diversity, Inc.: The Failed Promise of a Billion-Dollar Business* (New York: PublicAffairs, 2019).

10. Michael Ellison, "This Is How Big Tech Is Failing Its Black Employees," *Fast Company,* October 21, 2020.

11. Bob Moser, "The Reckoning of Morris Dees and the Southern Poverty Law Center," *New Yorker,* March 21, 2019.

12. Victor Ray, "A Theory of Racialized Organizations," *American Sociological Review* 84, no. 1 (February 2019): 26–53.

13. Malcolm X and Alex Haley, *The Autobiography of Malcolm X* (New York: Grove Press, 1965).

14. William Julius Wilson, *When Work Disappears: The World of the New Urban Poor* (New York: Vintage Books, 1996).

15. Adam Storer, Daniel Schneider, and Kristen Harknett, "What Explains Racial/Ethnic Inequality in Job Quality in the Service Sector?" *American Sociological Review* 85, no. 4 (August 2020): 537–72.

16. Margaret May Chin, *Stuck: Why Asian Americans Don't Reach the Top of the Corporate Ladder* (New York: NYU Press, 2020).

17. Ruha Benjamin, *Race After Technology: Abolitionist Tools for the New Jim Code* (Cambridge, UK: Polity Press, 2019).

18. Ruha Benjamin, "Assessing Risk, Automating Racism," *Science* 366, no. 6464 (October 25, 2019): 421–22.

19. Ziad Obermeyer, Brian Powers, Christine Vogeli, and Sendhil Mullainathan, "Dissecting Racial Bias in an Algorithm Used to Manage the Health of Populations," *Science* 366, no. 6464 (October 25, 2019): 447–53.

20. Kevin Stainback and Donald Tomaskovic-Devey, *Documenting Desegregation: Racial and Gender Segregation in Private Sector Employ-*

ment Since the Civil Rights Act (New York: Russell Sage Foundation, 2012).

21. Lauren A. Rivera, *Pedigree: How Elite Students Get Elite Jobs* (Princeton, NJ: Princeton University Press, 2015).

22. Lauren B. Edelman, Linda H. Krieger, Scott R. Eliason, Catherine R. Albiston, and Virginia Mellema, "When Organizations Rule: Judicial Deference to Institutionalized Employment Structures," *American Journal of Sociology* 117, no. 3 (November 2011): 888–954.

CHAPTER 9

1. Quoted in Patricia Hill Collins, *Intersectionality as Critical Social Theory* (Durham, NC: Duke University Press, 2019), 25. (Kindle edition)

2. Jessie Daniels, *Nice White Ladies: The Truth About White Supremacy, Our Role in It, and How We Can Help Dismantle It* (New York: Basic Books, 2021), 29.

3. Taylor Branch, *Parting the Waters: America in the King Years 1954–63* (New York: Simon & Schuster, 2007).

4. John D'Emilio, *Lost Prophet: The Life and Times of Bayard Rustin* (New York: Free Press, 2003).

5. Martin Luther King Jr., "Letter from Birmingham Jail," *Atlantic Monthly* 212, no. 2 (1963): 78–88.

6. Kimberlé Crenshaw, "Demarginalizing the Intersection of Race and Sex: A Black Feminist Critique of Antidiscrimination Doctrine, Feminist Theory and Antiracist Politics," *University of Chicago Legal Forum* 139 (1989).

7. Kimberlé Crenshaw, "Mapping the Margins: Intersectionality, Identity Politics, and Violence Against Women of Color," *Stanford Law Review* 43, no. 6 (1990): 1241–99.

8. Quoted in Avtar Brah and Ann Phoenix, "Ain't I a Woman? Revisiting Intersectionality," *Journal of International Women's Studies* 5, no. 3 (2004): 75–86, 77.

9. Zandria Felice Robinson, "Intersectionality," in *Handbook of Contemporary Sociological Theory*, ed. Seth Abrutyn, Handbooks of Sociology and Social Research (Cham, Switzerland: Springer, 2016), 477–99.

10. Ibid.

11. Martin Luther King Jr., *The Radical King* (Boston: Beacon Press, 2015), 250. (Kindle edition)

12. Keeanga-Yamahtta Taylor, ed., *How We Get Free: Black Feminism and the Combahee River Collective* (Chicago: Haymarket Books, 2017), 15.

13. Masha Gessen, *Surviving Autocracy* (New York: Riverhead, 2020).

14. Ben Shapiro is quoted and discussed by Jane Coaston in "The Intersectionality Wars," *Vox*, May 20, 2019.

Chapter 10

1. Martin Luther King Jr., *The Radical King* (Boston: Beacon Press, 2015), 238. (Kindle edition)

2. Peggy McIntosh, "White Privilege: Unpacking the Invisible Knapsack," in *Race, Class, and Gender in the United States: An Integrated Study* (New York: Worth, 2007): 177–82.

3. Tal Fortgang, "Why I'll Never Apologize for My White Male Privilege," *Time*, May 14, 2014.

4. Michael I. Norton and Samuel R. Sommers, "Whites See Racism as a Zero-Sum Game That They Are Now Losing," *Perspectives on Psychological Science* 6, no. 3 (2011): 215–18.

5. Keeanga-Yamahtta Taylor, ed., *How We Get Free: Black Feminism and the Combahee River Collective* (Chicago: Haymarket Books, 2017).

6. Here, I'll just note my Vassar professor's quip, "People who believe in 'reverse racism' think there is a right direction for it."

7. Barbara Smith, "I Helped Coin the Term 'Identity Politics.' I'm Endorsing Bernie Sanders," *The Guardian*, February 10, 2020.

8. Kimberlé Crenshaw, "Mapping the Margins: Intersectionality,

Identity Politics, and Violence Against Women of Color," *Stanford Law Review* 43, no. 6 (1991): 1241–99.

9. Olúfẹ́mi O. Táíwò, "Identity Politics and Elite Capture," *Boston Review,* May 7, 2020.

10. Derrick Bell, *Silent Covenants: Brown v. Board of Education and the Unfulfilled Hopes for Racial Reform* (New York: Oxford University Press, 2004).

11. Michelle Alexander, *The New Jim Crow: Mass Incarceration in the Age of Colorblindness* (New York: New Press, 2012).

12. Victor Ray, "Why Did Companies Take So Long to Divest from White Supremacy?" *Harvard Business Review,* January 25, 2021.

13. Charles W. Mills, *The Racial Contract* (Ithaca, NY: Cornell University Press, 1997), 138.

14. David R. Roediger, *The Wages of Whiteness: Race and the Making of the American Working Class* (New York: Verso, 1999).

15. Arlie Russell Hochschild, *Strangers in Their Own Land: Anger and Mourning on the American Right* (New York: New Press, 2016).

16. Angus Deaton and Anne Case, *Deaths of Despair and the Future of Capitalism* (Princeton, NJ: Princeton University Press, 2020).

17. Ta-Nehisi Coates, *We Were Eight Years in Power: An American Tragedy* (New York: One World, 2017), 350.

18. Lawrence B. Glickman, "The Racist Politics of the English Language," *Boston Review,* November 20, 2018.

19. Don Moynihan, "Bullshit, Branding and CRT," *Can We Still Govern?* (blog), October 2, 2021.

20. Malcolm X and Alex Haley, *The Autobiography of Malcolm X* (New York: Grove Press, 1965).

CONCLUSION

1. Carter G. Woodson, *The Mis-education of the Negro* (San Diego: Book Tree, 2006 [1933]), 84–85.

2. Kimberlé Crenshaw, Neil Gotanda, Gary Peller, and Kendall Thomas, eds., *Critical Race Theory: The Key Writings That Formed the Movement* (New York: New Press, 1996).

3. Richard Delgado and Jean Stefancic, *Critical Race Theory: An Introduction,* 2nd ed. (New York: NYU Press, 2012).

4. W.E.B. Du Bois, "The Souls of White Folk," in *Darkwater: Voices from Within the Veil* (New York: Dover, 2012).

5. Richard Rothstein, *The Color of Law: A Forgotten History of How Our Government Segregated America* (New York: Liveright, 2017).

6. Charles W. Mills, *The Racial Contract,* 25th anniversary ed. (Ithaca, NY: Cornell University Press, 2022).

7. David Levering Lewis and W.E.B. Du Bois, *Black Reconstruction in America: An Essay Toward a History of the Part Which Black Folk Played in the Attempt to Reconstruct Democracy in America, 1860-1880,* The Oxford W.E.B. Du Bois (New York: Oxford University Press, 2014). (Kindle edition)

INDEX

ABOUT THE AUTHOR

Victor Ray was born in Pittsburgh and raised in western Pennsylvania. After earning his bachelor of arts in urban studies at Vassar, he earned his PhD from Duke University in 2014. His work has been published in a number of peer-reviewed journals, including *American Sociological Review* and *The Annals of the American Academy of Political and Social Science,* and has won multiple awards, including the Distinguished Early Career Award from the American Sociological Association's Section on Racial and Ethnic Minorities and the Society for the Study of Social Problems Kimberlé Crenshaw Outstanding Article Award. Dr. Ray is a Nonresident Senior Fellow at the Brookings Institution, and his research has been funded by the Ford Foundation. As an active public scholar, he has written social and critical commentary for outlets such as *The Washington Post, Harvard Business Review,* CNN Opinion, *FiveThirtyEight,* and *Boston Review.* Dr. Ray currently resides in Iowa City, Iowa.

Twitter: @victorerikray

ABOUT THE TYPE

This book was set in Dante, a typeface designed by Giovanni Mardersteig (1892–1977). Conceived as a private type for the Officina Bodoni in Verona, Italy, Dante was originally cut only for hand composition by Charles Malin, the famous Parisian punch cutter, between 1946 and 1952. Its first use was in an edition of Boccaccio's *Trattatello in laude di Dante* that appeared in 1954. The Monotype Corporation's version of Dante followed in 1957. Though modeled on the Aldine type used for Pietro Cardinal Bembo's treatise *De Aetna* in 1495, Dante is a thoroughly modern interpretation of that venerable face.